THE 10 COMMANDMENTS FOR EVERYDAY LIVING

Bible principles for living life by the book!

By Rev. Dr. Trevor Udennis D.D.
Copyright © 2012 Trevor H Udennis
All rights reserved.
ISBN-10: 0-9564906-1-1
ISBN-13: 978-0-9564906-1-2

Author: Dr. Trevor H. Udennis D.D.

First published in the UK by EasyRway Ltd in 2012
1st Edition 2012

www.DrTrevorUdennis.com

www.pillar.org.uk

Copyright © 2012 by Rev. Dr. Trevor H. Udennis D.D.

The rights of Trevor Udennis to be identified as the author of this work have been asserted in accordance with the Copyright, Designs and patents Act 1988

ISBN: 978-0-9564906-1-2

DEDICATION

I would like to thank God for giving me an opportunity to bless His people and I ask Him to use this teaching to be a blessing to others even as He has used it to be a blessing to me and my family. I dedicate this work to my dear wife Julia and the sons of our fruitful union Theron & Danel.

CONTENTS

		Pages
	Acknowledgments	7
	Introduction	9
1	The 10 Commandments	15
2	The law of idolatry explained	31
3	The law of faithfulness explained	41
4	The law of Sabbath explained	55
5	The law of respect explained	85
6	The law of preservation explained	93
7	The law of faithfulness explained	101
8	The laws of honesty and authenticity	113
9	The law of satisfaction explained	121
10	The foundation of the Law	129
11	A new thing from an old thing	149
12	The limitation of the first Covenant	177
13	The Sabbath Home Bible Study	189
14	A question of Sabbath	221

ACKNOWLEDGMENTS

I give all glory to God without whose inspiration this book would not have been possible. I thank him for opening my understanding when I could have been a, "such were some of you" for this I truly give God thanks.

Having understood this subject more perfectly I am now able to share with others what the Lord has taught me through men and by direct inspiration. To God and God alone be the Glory.

When God lines up scripture line upon line and precept upon precept it is at this point that the hungry heart can find rest and contentment. Knowing that the scripture can never lie, we are able to say that we have found the truth.

We all must come to the place where we lay down our opinions and let God be true. When we do this we arrive at a place of peace and harmony with the scripture that questioning does not shake.

I would like to thank my wife Julia and my two boys Theron and Danel for their patience and understanding. I have a wonderful wife and marvellous children, and I know that a pastor's family makes many silent sacrifices and for this no one can repay them but God. "May the Lord richly bless you with His grace according to your needs. I love you!"

I would like to thank Sis. Elaine Lamaswala for her willingness to type and photocopy the initial book a long time ago, commonly known as "once upon a time". Who would have thought there would have been a revision and expansion of that original work? God is good.

My heart felt thanks goes out to Pastor Christine Dormer who worked as my secretary during this project. I thank you for your boundless enthusiasm in typing, formatting and offering constructive ideas as to how this book could best serve its purpose. You are greatly appreciated; this book would not have happened yet, had the Lord not given you 'the want to'. Thanks!

Sincere thanks go out to Bishop HC McFarlane for the solid foundation of doctrine he has transmitted to me as a heritage, for my grooming in the ministry and for everything he has done and given as a spiritual father for and to me.

Special thanks go out to my friend, discussion partner, and chief editor Brother Delroy Gayle. Without his human input none of this work would be of the quality and standard that it is. It was mainly his influence as a human channel that God has used to bring about the inspiration and development of this work. "My friend God has blessed you with a quick and powerfully analytical mind. So make full proof of your ministry." This work is a tribute to his research into this subject more than to any single factor I can think of; may God richly bless you!

Finally I would like to thank all of the Saints at the **'Pillar of Faith Church'** who are so supportive of the ministry which the Lord has given us and who are faithful in their various departments. For your time, for your prayers, for your giving and for your living I thank you.

To Sis. Kerry Walker for the proof reading and Bro. John Matthews for his involvement in this project. To all the other dear friends too numerous to mention in this small work – Thank you and may God bless you all.

Introduction

So why another book on the subject of the law and Sabbath? Well the purpose of this book is actually very simple. This book is not written for those who are not hungry; it is not for those who do not want to have their perceptions challenged.

This book is written in order to answer some of the questions that have troubled sincere Bible believers who have a desire to understand the subject matter covered within these pages.

If you sincerely wish to understand the subject of Sabbath then you are in the right place. If you sincerely want to understand the relationship between the law and grace, then read on. If you seek to gain insight into the application of the law to your life today and its relevance to the modern man then this is the book for you.

My secondary desire is to equip believers by enabling them to bring clarity to the minds of other sincere seekers of truth to whom God allows them the privilege of ministering.

Everything that God has said or does in the scripture is based upon a principle, and is repeated in a clear pattern for our sound understanding. We can be sure, God never changes His principles, **Hebrews 13:8** *"Jesus Christ **the same** yesterday, and to day, and for ever."* He only explains them so that we might understand and walk with Him in the light of clear revelation knowledge. He does not change because He is the same!

We should therefore seek to follow God in the full light of revelation and never be satisfied with our level of perception until we clearly understand and are able to give an enlightened biblical account to all that come seeking to know Him better.

1 Peter 3:15 *"But sanctify the Lord God in your hearts:* **<u>and be ready always to give an answer to every man</u>** *that asketh you a reason of the hope that is in you with meekness and fear:"*

Throughout the centuries, but more specifically since the late 1800's there has been much controversy, about certain applications of the Law, which is also called the 10 Commandments or the "ten words". The main focus of the controversy has developed around the fourth commandment. This is the one about the Sabbath or more pointedly the seventh day of the week.

However I need to point out even at this early stage that the Sabbath did not just pertain to a day of the week, but Israel had to keep Sabbaths (plural). There were Sabbath weeks, months and years. The ultimate of which was the year of Jubilee. Sabbath was a generic word that had a lot of applications in scripture, but its meaning was always the same – Rest *or "Sabbath - always means* **REST** *it just never changes."*

Many questions have traditionally been left unanswered on 'the issue of the law', (this includes the Sabbath) and as a consequence of the unanswered questions, much misunderstanding has arisen around the subject of the Law and its relationship to Sabbath keeping and Sabbath keepers.

The misunderstanding of the scriptures concerning the revelation of the law; has led to the deception of many sincere people of God and countless seekers of truth who genuinely want God's best for themselves and others, but took a wrong turning at some point in their search for truth.

The devil has used the ignorance demonstrated by many, concerning the topic of the Law to cause many denominational splits, and the formation of numerous organisations and 'isms'.

Like any Biblical subject matter, the law can be understood and misunderstood. However we must remain objective and come without preconceived ideas and let the Bible speak to us. The Bible is indeed its own best interpreter.

Every subject will unfold it-self before us if we diligently seek to understand and do not distort or bend scriptures that we do not understand or which do not fit neatly into our doctrinal frame work.

Doctrinally some people are like the man who bought his furniture and then went out to purchase a house that had the exact dimensions to fit his furnishings into.

Even the most self-opinionated person knows the correct way to go about such a transaction is to buy a house that suits your needs and then shop for furnishings that will complement the home you have purchased.

The Bible is the house that meets all your needs and doctrine must complement what is in the Bible. We should not expect the Bible to accommodate our pet doctrines. Instead our pet doctrines should be vetted, limited and corrected by what the Bible says.

Firstly we should seek to find out what the Bible says, and then we should seek to understand whether what we think we understand is accurately measurable in relationship to all the Bible has to say on that subject.

When you have done these with understanding then what you have found is truth. Truth doesn't mind being questioned, but it will always give you the same answer in any given set of circumstances. Truth is consistent and truth is revealing.

As I have said, the Law is often misunderstood, but it is very important that we have a clear understanding because of the day and time that we are living in.

In fact I would view the particular religious inclination towards the law that is displayed in this present day period as one of 'denial'.

Modern day observance of the law denies the purpose and work of Christ unless the law is viewed from the correct biblical perspective. The thing about the Law is that it must be understood, because understanding this topic is a matter of bondage and liberty.

It is important to notice that those who believe in the observance of the Law at times see the Sabbath (or law) as being the only way for a person to be saved. This is in spite of the fact that this was not what Jesus or His apostles taught as the original Bible plan of salvation.

Read their words when the dispute arose among them as to whether or not Gentiles should keep any aspects of the law. **Acts 15:10** *"Now therefore why tempt ye God, to put a yoke upon the neck of the disciples, which neither our fathers nor we were able to bear? [11] But we believe that through the grace of the Lord Jesus Christ we shall be saved, even as they."*

I would go as far as to extend a challenge that, **"If you can find it in scripture where it is taught that the law is necessary for salvation in the New Testament period, then I would like to know about it"**.

Truly if I have missed something here then I need to know, because I have made up my mind to make heaven my home. So if you find it write me.

It is clear therefore that *those who believe in the law as the means of salvation do so in direct denial of the Holy scriptures*.

In scripture we see that when asked by the multitudes for the very first time in the New Testament age *"what shall we do to be saved"*, their was not a hint of a reference to the requirements of the law.

The model answer is found in **Acts Chapter 2 verse 38** and then throughout the remainder of the Bible this continues to be the answer given for salvation. The pattern for the original New Testament salvation as preached by the disciples of Jesus Christ is very consistent.

Acts 2:38 *"Then Peter said unto them, Repent, and be baptized every one of you in the name of Jesus Christ for the remission of sins, and ye shall receive the gift of the Holy Ghost."*

Acts 8:14 *"Now when the apostles which were at Jerusalem heard that Samaria had received the word of God, they sent unto them Peter and John:*
[15] Who, when they were come down, prayed for them, that they might receive the Holy Ghost:
[16] (For as yet he was fallen upon none of them: only they were baptized in the name of the Lord Jesus.)
[17] Then laid they their hands on them, and they received the Holy Ghost".

In the scripture below the ministry of the word of salvation goes out to Gentiles for the first time and this is a special occasion which will set the stage for every Gentile Christian for the rest of the ages. Let's examine closely the instructions and see if there is any reference to keeping the Law?

Acts 10:44 *"While Peter yet spake these words, the Holy Ghost fell on all them which heard the word.*
[45] And they of the circumcision which believed were astonished, as many as came with Peter, because that on the Gentiles also was poured out the gift of the Holy Ghost.
[46] For they heard them speak with tongues, and magnify God. Then answered Peter,
[47] Can any man forbid water, that these should not be baptized, which have received the Holy Ghost as well as we?
[48] And he commanded them to be baptized in the name of the Lord. Then prayed they him to tarry certain days".

The above mentioned scriptures are the Biblical facts of how people got saved in the Bible and there are no references to keeping the law either as an essential or a complement to salvation. This means that anything else as a means of salvation is mere fiction and therefore not necessary.

The scriptures cannot be broken; if God saves one person in the New Testament time period one way He will save all that way. Because He repeats the salvation message and salvation method over and over again, we can be assured that this is the right way to be saved.

If God chose to give us alternative means of salvation, it would not be consistent with His character and it would be confusing; and we know that God is not the author of confusion.

> **We can say from our brief examination thus far, that the correct understanding of the law is a matter of bondage or Liberty. Scripture admonishes you to choose life!**

CHAPTER 1

THE TEN COMMANDMENTS

Let's begin our observations by going to the book of Exodus Chapter 20 and look at what the Bible has to say. We are looking into **what are the Ten Commandments and law?** *What do we mean when we say 'the Ten Commandments'?*

The uninformed often refer to the Bible as being written by men. This is true in respect to who actually did the writing, but the Bible says that the scriptures were given by inspiration of God in **2 Timothy 3:16** and that these precepts were not the results of any man's private interpretation is confirmed in **2 Peter 1:21**. But the Ten Commandments were originally written by God Himself. Therefore the Ten Commandments are not and have never been the Ten Suggestions. Obedience to these commandments were to bring blessings; and disobedience was to bring about a curse.

Let us therefore carefully consider the Ten Commandments. *Exodus 20:1-20 And* **God spoke all these words,** *saying: 2 "I am the LORD your God, who brought you out of the land of Egypt, out of the house of bondage.*

3 "You shall have no other gods before Me.

4 "You shall not make for yourself a carved image, or any likeness of anything that is in heaven above, or that is in the earth beneath, or that is in the water under the earth;

5 you shall not bow down to them nor serve them. For I, the LORD your God, am a jealous God, visiting the iniquity of the fathers on the children to the third and fourth generations of those who hate Me,

6 but showing mercy to thousands, to those who love Me and keep My commandments.

7 "You shall not take the name of the LORD your God in vain, for the LORD will not hold him guiltless who takes His name in vain.

8 "Remember the Sabbath day, to keep it holy.

9 Six days you shall labour and do all your work,

10 but the seventh day is the Sabbath of the LORD your God. In it you shall do no work: you, nor your son, nor your daughter, nor your male servant, nor your female servant, nor your cattle, nor your stranger who is within your gates.

11 For in six days the LORD made the heavens and the earth, the sea, and all that is in them, and rested the seventh day. Therefore the LORD blessed the Sabbath day and hallowed it.

12 "Honour your father and your mother, that your days may be long upon the land which the LORD your God is giving you.

13 "You shall not murder.

14 "You shall not commit adultery.

15 "You shall not steal.

16 "You shall not bear false witness against your neighbour. 17 "You shall not covet your neighbour's house; you shall not covet your neighbour's wife, nor his male servant, nor his female servant, nor his ox, nor his donkey, nor anything that is your neighbour's.

God outlines His Commandments in the above scriptures, and I have tried to break them down so that we can analyse them and hopefully understand them also.

Overview of the Ten Commandments
#1 You shall have no other gods before Me.
The surrounding nations had all sorts of gods that they worshipped and served. There was a god for any and everything one could imagine (war, fertility, death etc.).

Because bad company corrupts good morals God warned them against thee kind of company they should keep and the kind of God they should worship.

Just because we live in a fallen world does not mean we have to practice its sinful ways. How can we transgress this commandment?

By putting any other thing before God Almighty. This can be our own pride, our possessions, our money, and our lusts.

Whatever we depend on more than God can become a god to us, and that is NOT what God wants!

#2 *You shall not make for yourself a carved image.*
God will not be worshiped with statues, idols, pictures, or any other religious symbol. God is a spirit, and is not housed in a body made by men. To set up statues conveys just the opposite of the way it really is-- that God is infinite, almighty, and is spirit. God is approached by faith, not by images.

#3 You shall not take the name of the LORD your God in vain.
When you profess Christ, yet live in hypocrisy, you are taking God's name in vain. Those that name the name of Christ yet do not forsake their wicked ways, but continue to practice sin, are guilty of this commandment. Take God serious, and purpose to live for Him, and really mean it!

#4 Remember the Sabbath day, to keep it holy.
The example goes all the way back to creation. God finished the work of creation in six days, and on the seventh He rested. The physical benefits to resting one day a week are well documented.

The spiritual renewal that can take place is also proven in those who seek the Lord and His service on this Sabbath day also. It is so beneficial that God included it in the Ten Commandments!

 #5 Honour your father and your mother.
This is noted as the first commandment with a promise, and that promise is a long life! Jesus also referred to this commandment **Matthew chapter 15**. Whether or not your parents were good to you is not the issue.

Your part is to honour them, and in so doing God will command His blessing to be upon you. *It is so very important for a Christian to honour their parents!*

#6 You shall not murder.
Matthew Henry's commentary says: "*You shall not do any thing hurtful or injurious to the health, ease, and life of your own body, or any other person's unjustly.*

It does not forbid killing in lawful war, or in our own necessary defence, but it forbids all malice and hatred to the person of any, and all personal revenge arising therefrom."

However, self-harm, murder, and violence to others is fully covered under this definition and means that anyone who takes the life of another without good cause e.g. self-defence, is a murderer and under the law was worthy of death.

#7 You shall not commit adultery.
If this commandment was obeyed, their would be, for the most part, no AIDS crisis and no abortion issue. God warned man, but men chose to go their own way and thus we have our current situation.

This sin defiles the body and will lead to heartache and destruction as sure as if we inflicted physical injury to ourselves.

#8 You shall not steal.
This does not need much explanation. Stealing is wrong. It is an invasion of another's labour.

It violates the supreme law that one must work for what they have, or be given possessions by a benevolent person or persons. Again, stealing is wrong.

#9 You shall not bear false witness against your neighbour.
One must not lie to others, or attempt even to deceive them. Racial slurs are also wrong from this commandment.

Slandering, gossiping, backbiting; trying to raise one's own reputation at the expense of another is a breach of this commandment.

#10 You shall not covet.
This commandment forbids the lusting after that which is rightfully someone else's. Whether it is someone else's wife, property, position, or possessions, we must not covet after them.

These are inordinate desires that need to be brought to Christ so that we can be cleansed and forgiven, and given divine strength to overcome a covetous attitude.

So why did God give the Ten Commandments?
The Bible says in **1 John 5:3,** *For this is the love of God, that we keep his commandments: and his commandments are not grievous (burdensome).*

In the same T*wentieth chapter of Exodus*, just following the Ten Commandments, Moses says to the people: "*Do not fear; for God has come to test you, and that His fear may be before you, **so that you may not sin.**"*

God's commandments are given for us to live better lives before Him with whom we have to do **Hebrews 4:13**. They are for our benefit, so that we may not sin, so that we will better know His love and nearness.

The bottom line is that God had just delivered Israel out of Egypt and out of the hands of the Egyptians, and they were in the wilderness at a place called Horeb and at a Mountain called Sinai. The Bible seems to interchangeably use Horeb sometimes and other times it says Sinai.

In Exodus Chapter 19, and I am reading from verse 3 the Bible says, *"And Moses went up unto God, and the LORD called unto him out of the mountain, saying, Thus shalt thou say to The house of Jacob, and tell the children of Israel* (below)
Exodus 19:4 *Ye have seen what I did unto the Egyptians, and how I bare you on eagles' wings, and brought you unto myself.*

*[5] Now therefore, if ye will obey **my voice indeed, and keep my Covenant**, then ye shall be a **peculiar treasure** unto me above all people: for all the earth is mine:*

*[6] And ye shall be unto me **a kingdom of priests, and an holy nation**. These are the words which thou shalt **speak unto the children of Israel**."* (Compare verses 4 and 5 with *1 Peter 2:9*).

Then God told Moses to get the people ready; He told him to sanctify the people, He commanded him to sanctify the mountain; He told him to put bounds round the mountain because He didn't want the people coming near the mountain.

He said: *"When my presence comes upon this mountain, My mountain will be a holy mountain. So don't let a solitary beast, or a single animal get near this mountain."* God was about to make what we call a covenant. God was about to meet His people.

Now what is a covenant?
A covenant is a contract; a formal legal agreement that is legally binding; an agreement between two parties or between man and mankind or between man and God. It can even be between man and the spiritual powers of the darkness.

It is a contract, agreement, pact or compact. The Hebrew word for Covenant also means to cut. It comes from a Hebrew word which carries the idea of cutting in the way that you may have heard of concerning the ancient ceremonies of blood brothers.

A part of the ceremony would require both parties to cut their thumbs (or other parts of the body – usually the hand or arm) and put them together and make a bonding contract through this act of exchanging blood.

This would be symbolic of their blood now being one. It would mean my life has become your life and yours mine. It was a way of saying *"Your blood is my blood, your life is my life, your world is my world and your interests are my interests."*

So God was going to cut an agreement; He was about to make a contract with the people of Israel. So He set the limits round the mountain in order that no one would go up the mountain uninvited and therefore die.

Moses went up into the mountain because he was invited and there God began to speak forth the terms of the contract.

In **Exodus Chapter 20** (an extract of which is written above) God records the momentous occasion when He began to speak to Israel and He starts by saying these ten special commandments which are symbolic of the 613 precepts (points) of the law.

These we call the Ten Commandments. At this point, we will take a look into each of the 10 Commandments and how they apply to our lives today. We will also briefly indicate something of how they were applied in their original context.

Before we move immediately to law number one here is a Summary thought:

> A singular part of the Law is symbolic of the whole, but it is the whole or entire law that is important and not just the parts. The six hundred and thirteen points are symbolic of the entire law of which the Sabbath is but a one point.
>
> However it is amazing that whole religions and denominations have been built around this one aspect of the Law as though it was independent and more important than the rest of God's Word.
>
> It isn't so get over it! God's Word is one and all of it is important, and we must balance all of it by understanding what God is saying in the mouth of two or three witnesses.

LAW NUMBER 1 - THE LAW OF ONE GOD

Exodus 20:3 Thou shalt have no other gods before me.

This is the first law it is one that is written against polytheism, that is, believing in more than one God. This requires the acknowledging of only one true and living God. This is monotheism, to have only one God.

The God of Israel is the one God of the Bible. He is the one God of the known and unknown universe, and He won't take second place to anyone. He will not play second fiddle for anyone, He is the one and only true God. He is the first, the last and the only God.

This law stresses the singleness of God and His sovereign majesty. God is a God of communication. He let's us know the situation as it is. There is only one God and it's the Lord.

There can be no other God beside Him. He rightfully claims first place in our lives and refuses to share us with any other God. The essence of God's command to love Him is to be so in love with Him that our affections for other things are like hate in comparison to our love towards him.

Luke 14:26 "If any man come to me, and hate not his father, and mother, and wife, and children, and brethren, and sisters, yea, and his own life also, he cannot be my disciple. "This scripture is so subtle that you can miss it. You need to read it again!"

The rich young ruler is the clearest biblical example of someone who felt he loved God and upon closer examination had another God. When he said that he had fulfilled the law from a child, Jesus did not argue with him.

He simply asked him to do something that would reveal the nature of his true problem. This young man had a problem he had another god in his life. Unwilling to give up his other god, he went away sorrowful. Now you and I can be just as sure that today, God won't share you with another god.

Luke 18:18 "*And a certain ruler asked him, saying, Good Master, what shall I do to inherit eternal life?*
[19] And Jesus said unto him, Why callest thou me good? none is good, save one, that is, God.
[20] Thou knowest the commandments, Do not commit adultery, Do not kill, Do not steal, Do not bear false witness, Honour thy father and thy mother.
[21] And he said, All these have I kept from my youth up.
[22] Now when Jesus heard these things, he said unto him, Yet lackest thou one thing: sell all that thou hast, and distribute unto the poor, and thou shalt have treasure in heaven: and come, follow me.
[23] And when he heard this, he was very sorrowful: for he was very rich."

Yes the rich young ruler had another god, because his heart was in love with another. Hear God's advice on the matter. **Psalms 62:10** "*Trust not in oppression, and become not vain in robbery: if riches increase, set not your heart upon them.*"

Obviously his heart was totally identified with the wealth of this world to the point where he did not see the value of the wealth of the world to come that he met that day. He rejected Jesus for money.

It was Adam's love for Eve that paved the slippery way to sin which the human race now walks. Adam appears to have loved Eve above God. I believe that Adam made up his mind that he would rather die as God had said, than lose 'the bone of his bone and flesh of his flesh' now that he had her.

He was not deceived; the Bible tells us this, 1 **Timothy 2:13-14** *"For Adam was first formed, then Eve. And Adam was not deceived, but the woman being deceived was in the transgression."* This means that Adam made a deliberate choice to sin against God.

He actually chose Eve above God. Instead he should have chosen God above himself and Eve. How many times have we been guilty of this, choosing other things before God? That's the Adamic trait at work.

As a result of that original sin (That is, Adam's love) continues in the remainder of mankind. We now continue in actions of sin, which God calls rebellion. Through these acts of sin, we show who is really the god of our life.

Romans 5:12 *"Wherefore, as by one man sin entered into the world, and death by sin; and so death passed upon all men, for that all have sinned:"*

Our actions are the indicators that show just what we really do love. You only have to look at what you do with your time, talents and money to see what you really worship.

Actions speak louder than words. Is your God your belly? Now that will show, won't it? And lots of pastors said – Amen.

Whose praise do we speak most and seek most? Do you love God with a passion – then tell me what do you do with your time? Who has your time, T.V. or God? During what activity and in what place do you have the most fun?

If the answers with the thoughts that rush into your mind after the last question about activity aren't about spiritual pursuit of God in some way, and if the place is not linked to His presence, then you have a problem. You have another god.

If we were to take an inventory of your mind, what would we find you thinking about most? Is it cars, fashion, cookery, house or housing, school or schooling, computer games perhaps?

Do you think your life gives God pleasure; He said of Jesus,"*This is my beloved son in whom I am well pleased.*" Could He say that of you and the places you go?

Do you love others, and give your self in His service sacrificially? Are you given to gossip, pride, self-exhalation, envy, jealousy, and hypocrisy? Are you motivated to do well by guilt and not because of love? You may have another god.

The million pound question is, do you have another god lurking in the hidden recesses of your life? Ask yourself; is God really first in my life? Have I been putting anyone or anything before God and my service of Him?

How about family, friends, work, leisure, other interests? How about your own opinions? This is the first commandment – Love God with all of your being. After your whole being, there isn't a lot of room for anything else is there?

Mark 12:29 *"And Jesus answered him; the first of all the Commandments is, Hear, O Israel; The Lord our God is one Lord:*

[30] And thou shalt love the Lord thy God with all thy heart, and with all thy soul, and with all thy mind, and with all thy strength: this is the first commandment.

[31]And the second is like, namely this, Thou shalt love thy neighbour as thyself. There is none other commandment greater than these.

[32]And the scribe said unto him, Well, Master, thou hast said the truth: for there is one God; and there is none other but he:"

LOVE GOD WITH ALL OF YOUR BEING AND AFTER THAT THERE IS NO ROOM FOR ANY OTHER LOVES!

> **God will not tolerate any secret loves. You can have Him and *no other lover*. You are not supposed to have any other love in your life but God. To love Him with everything you have is the first of all commandments.**

CHAPTER 2

The law of idolatry explained as the law of purity of heart – law number 2

Exodus 20:4-6 Thou shalt not make unto thee any graven image, or any likeness of any thing that is in heaven above, or that is in the earth beneath, or that is in the water under the earth: Thou shalt not bow down thyself to them, nor serve them: for I the LORD thy God am a jealous God, visiting the iniquity of the fathers upon the children unto the third and fourth generation of them that hate me; And showing mercy unto thousands of them that love me, and keep my Commandments.

This then was **the law against idolatry**. God specifically ordered Israel, not to make any graven image neither to bow down to them. Now when God says don't bow to any graven image, He means **don't bow**. Even if you think it's the mother of the man Jesus Christ, don't bow.

You shouldn't bow to any images, statues, icons, nor any form or representation of God. No angel or man, no demon spirit nor anything else deserves our worship. None but God is to be worshiped.

You simply must not bow, you can refuse to bow. God made a law against idolatry because He is a Spirit and has no form. Since He has no form or image, nothing can adequately describe or represent Him.

He is in a class all by Himself; and does not like mankind to give glory to a mere image when they can worship the true and living God. As I have stated already, God is also the only being worthy of our homage. He exists to be worshipped and we were created to worship. We should bow to none but Him and Him alone. Worship God!

Have you made an image to represent God physically or in your heart? For instance when you pray do you have a form and feature you look at in your mind while praying to God?

Perhaps it is Michel-Angelo's blue eyed, blond long-haired Jesus? Or perhaps it is the Rastafarian Jesus that so many see in their minds. Incidentally Jesus was a Jew neither a European nor an African.

All idols are hateful to God because they rob Him of glory that is due only to Him. Whether the idols are physical or spiritual in nature, God feels the same about them all; He hates them with a passion.

God is a Spirit being and able to do all things by Himself. The idea that He needs help from any source is highly offensive to Him. God really does not need anyone. One of the main things about idols is they can do nothing.

God is not an idol, He can do anything He chooses to do; He is also not a limited physical being, so physical limitations simply do not apply to Him.

He is not a mind so mental gymnastics do not impress Him. Neither can we know Him by intellectual pursuit. So our IQ means nothing in His eyes. We can never get to the depths of fully understanding God, for God is far past searching out. God is all-powerful and fully in control.

God is not an emotion, so we will not always feel Him. God is not nature but rather its creator, therefore we cannot see Him. Though we can see God's handiwork in nature, it is important that we understand that God is not His creation.

God is a Spirit; He is higher, greater, more magnificent and glorious than His creation. God is the creator. God is an all knowing, all seeing, all-powerful, everywhere present, eternal Spirit. Don't worship any object you can see, touch or feel instead worship God.

Matthew 4:10 "Then saith Jesus unto him, Get thee hence, Satan: for it is written, Thou shalt worship the Lord thy God, and him only shalt thou serve."

There is no one else worthy, not one. The only individual we should worship is God. He gave us life, He calls the shots, and He is the boss. He alone is worthy to be worshipped. Everyone else is created, but He is the creator. Let us worship God.

Revelation 19:10 "And I fell at his feet to worship him. And he said unto me, See thou do it not: I am thy fellowservant, and of thy brethren that have the testimony of Jesus: worship God: for the testimony of Jesus is the spirit of prophecy."

We are not to bow to anyone except God in heaven and Jesus Christ His son who is 'God enfleshed'. God will not accept the worship of a divided heart; He must be the only love of our lives.

This is what God seeks and this is what we must bring. God is seeking to be Lord (master of our life and destiny) He seeks to be the only Lord, because the only Lord is what He is. Indeed there is but *'one Lord, one faith and one baptism."*

Matthew 6:24 "No man can serve two masters: for either he will hate the one, and love the other; or else he will hold to the one, and despise the other. Ye cannot serve God and mammon."

God refuses to be one among many Gods or even chief God among several, *Isaiah 42:8 "I am the LORD: that is my name: and my glory will I not give to another, neither my praise to graven images."*

Our duty to God is to love, worship and serve Him and Him alone. If you have any unresolved conflicts in your heart, you have another God, and you are committing the sin of idolatry.

> **Whatever comes before God in importance or priority in your mind and life is your God.**

If you have another god or graven image and you are dissatisfied, the real reason for your dissatisfaction is because poor substitutes can never satisfy, what you need is the real thing.

The real God and not a false god is the answer to the sin of idolatry. Check your life and make sure something hasn't stolen the real thing and left a counterfeit in your life. Like the Israelites of old, we must burn, break and destroy the counterfeits and cherish the real thing.

We do indeed have many modern day idols. Some are still in stone, e.g. the idols of the heathen and the Catholics. Others are in the mind of men who worship them. How about success, money, beauty, and popularity. All of these are key idols of our modern day times.

There are an endless number of gods that we have made in our own image. From the Greek and Roman gods of antiquity who were riddled with the same failures as the men that conceived them; to the bearded old man who sits in a picture reading to Adam?

Then there is man made religion with its millions of gods. From the animal gods of Egypt and Hinduism to the false images of bleeding heart Jesus' and bleeding heart Marys in home mantle pieces and fetishes on miniature crosses. Could this be another Jesus?

2 Corinthians 11:4 *"For if he that cometh preacheth another Jesus, whom we have not preached, or if ye receive another spirit, which ye have not received, or another gospel, which ye have not accepted, ye might well bear with him."*

The Jesus of the Bible was on a cross, but today He is risen – Hallelujah. We should be extra careful not to commit the sin of idolatry, for God warns us in His word that, *"He will by no means clear the guilty."* **Exodus 34:7**; Don't change the truth of God into a lie, **Romans 1:25.**

Multitudes today are making gods in their own images, when they ought to be praying to see God as He is. If you don't know Him, He stands ready to reveal Himself to you, why don't you simply ask Him to show you the truth about Himself.

Some say that God is just a God of Love. Nothing could be further from the truth. God is bigger than that, this is but half of the truth. It is therefore a false image; it gives people the wrong impression of God.

God is an awesome God and we need to see Him as He is. He is high and lifted up. Jesus Christ is Greater, more powerful and more important than His creation. He is the creator and we are the creatures.

Once this is established, we need no idols. Yes! He is a God of love, but He is also holy and righteous. He is unlike any other god that can be named or imagined. The main difference is that our God is a living god.

Psalms 115:2-8 *"Wherefore should the heathen say, Where is now their God?*

[3] But our God is in the heavens: he hath done whatsoever he hath pleased.

[4] *Their idols are silver and gold, the work of men's hands.*

[5] They have mouths, but they speak not: eyes have they, but they see not:

[6] They have ears, but they hear not: noses have they, but they smell not:

[7] They have hands, but they handle not: feet have they, but they walk not: neither speak they through their throat.

[8] They that make them are like unto them; so is every one that trusteth in them.

There are gods made with hands and gods made from the minds of men. There are only two perceptions of God possible. Either what you believe is Bible truth or it is a false image and an idol in your heart and therefore Bible error. Yes I am sure that the worst of all idols are opinions set in stone.

You may say you haven't made an image to represent God. But there are modern day images and idols created by men to represent God.

How about our opinions which are so often set in stone in a way that gives way to no one, not even the word of God? Opinions set in stone are front line idols. Our personal opinion can be a major barrier to communication between ourselves and God.

1 Samuel 15:23 "For rebellion is as the sin of witchcraft, and stubbornness is as iniquity and idolatry. Because thou hast rejected the word of the LORD, he hath also rejected thee from being king." Stubbornness is a form of idolatry, which means that the individual worships their own opinion".

Many people are in fact in love with their own opinions and this too is a form of Idolatry. **Colossians 3:5 says,** *"Mortify therefore your members which are upon the earth; fornication, uncleanness, inordinate affection, evil concupiscence, and covetousness, which is idolatry:"*

This particular verse says in essence that what soever we love we worship. Our cherished opinions can become our gods with very little effort on our part. Covetousness here refers to our personal highly cherished desires.

Humans are very clever. Sometimes we are clever to the point of deceiving ourselves into thinking ourselves cleverer than God. Us humans do not say there is no god, except for a few hard-nosed atheists, generally the average person does believe in 'something'.

We usually simply adopt a different strategy. We just deny God His rights as God. We behave as though He does not exist. Even while our conscience screams, we can pretend that there is no God and that we are in control.

Psalms 14:1 *To the chief Musician, A Psalm of David. The fool hath said in his heart, There is no God. They are corrupt, they have done abominable works, there is none that doeth good.*

Everything around us that we can see, teaches us that we are created beings that have been made. Nature teaches us there is a maker that created all things.

After accepting that there is a God, (or 'a something' as some would call Him); the next logical step for most humans who want things their own way (and yet who do accept that God does exist) is to live their lives while ignoring God.

There are three possible scenarios either we deny God fully or partially, ignore Him or believe in Him. God tells us in so many ways through His Word that the evidence to believe in Him is all around us. He tells us that those who do not believe in Him are without excuse.

There is no valid reason why anyone does not believe in God, because the evidence for His existence is all around us - **Romans 1:20**

Even though many know He is there, many continue to treat Him as though He does not exist, and therefore His commandments do not count. This is idolatry. To know yet pretend not to know (the true God) is a form of idolatry. I suppose it is fantasy and fantasy is a form of idolatry – by this I mean still doing things "my way". As you continue, soon "your way" becomes "your god".

Since He is our maker, He has the right to order us around and Lord it over us. Have you ever heard of a person who says, "I've always done it this way (meaning - 'my way') and I see no reason to change it now!" such a person is addicted to the "my way philosophy". This is idolatry and it is destructive.

Proverbs 14:12 "*There is a way which seemeth right unto a man, but the end thereof are <u>the ways of death</u>.*"

Translated into modern English that means, **'Your way will always end up killing you'**. Isn't it about time we try to do things God's way.

Instead of seeking to please God, we as humans have a way of making ourselves a personal god to suit our sins. A god that is going to be tolerant of our sins, rather than one that will judge our sin.

The sin of God denial makes God angry and provokes Him to jealousy. Further more it brings a curse up until the third to fourth generation. We need to avoid this, *John I 5:21* "*Little children, keep yourselves from idols. Amen.*"

Mankind must all come to realise that there is no God but the God of Israel, no God but the God of the Bible. All other gods are dead gods.

There is no God beside our God **Isaiah 44:8** *"Fear ye not, neither be afraid: have not I told thee from that time, and have declared it? ye are even my witnesses. Is there a God beside me? yea, there is no god; I know not any."*

Deuteronomy 6:4 *"Hear, O Israel: The LORD our God is one LORD:"* Anything but the one God of the Bible is an idol.

A heart free from idols is a heart prepared to be a temple of God - The Lord is the one God, but many prefer their opinions and their idols to submission and obedience to God.

> **Whatsoever we love, we worship. So we should love God and worship Him alone. Love for God will keep our heart idol free and worship-full.**

CHAPTER 3

The law of faithfulness explained as faithfulness to God's name – Law number 3

Exodus 20:7 *Thou shalt not take the name of the LORD thy God in vain; for the LORD will not hold him guiltless that taketh his name in vain.*

This command means we ought not to use God's name in a light or careless way, especially not for the purpose of cursing and swearing. Another way of describing misuse of the name of the Lord or "Yahweh" is blasphemy.

We must be very careful here. Jesus taught Hallowed be His name. That is to say God's name is holy. God will not continually permit careless use of His name, to do so is to be classified as an enemy of God.

Psalms 139:20 *"For they speak against thee wickedly, and thine enemies take thy name in vain."*

Some never call the words 'God' or the name Jesus, except it being used to curse and swear. Then they say, "I don't mean anything by it".

How would you feel if someone called you one of the filthiest things you could think of, and then told you they meant nothing by it? The excuse would be unacceptable wouldn't it? Well that's how God feels about blasphemy!

Some say it is simply a habit. Well I say it's a bad habit of showing disrespect and dishonour to God that must stop. The remedy to cursing and swearing is loving God with all your being.

Psalms 19:14 *"Let the words of my mouth, and the meditation of my heart, **be acceptable in thy sight**, O LORD, my strength, and my redeemer".*

Our words are the simplest and most effective way we can show contempt for God. We can do this by abusing His name. But one who fears God will never use His name disrespectfully and never accept the disrespect of others to God's name either.

After the fall of mankind into sin, men knew the name of the Lord. Then later through disuse and neglect men ceased to call on that name until the days of Seth.

Genesis 4:26 *"And to Seth, to him also there was born a son; and he called his name Enos: **then began men to call upon the name of the LORD.**"*

After the flood, the knowledge of God continued in the Earth for a short time, up until shortly after the dispersion of men at Babel. At this time they took the knowledge of God with them, but it did not take too long before man began to worship the creature instead of the Creator.

Romans 1:20 *"For the invisible things of him from the creation of the world are clearly seen, being understood by the things that are made, even his eternal power and Godhead; so that they are without excuse:*

[21] Because that, when they knew God, they glorified him not as God, neither were thankful; but became vain in their imaginations, and their foolish heart was darkened.

[22] Professing themselves to be wise, they became fools,

[23] And changed the glory of the uncorruptible God into an image made like to corruptible man, and to birds, and fourfooted beasts, and creeping things.

[24] Wherefore God also gave them up to uncleanness through the lusts of their own hearts, to dishonour their own bodies between themselves:

[25] Who changed the truth of God into a lie, and worshipped and served the creature more than the Creator, who is blessed for ever. Amen.

[26] For this cause God gave them up unto vile affections: for even their women did change the natural use into that which is against nature:

[27] And likewise also the men, leaving the natural use of the woman, burned in their lust one toward another; men with men working that which is unseemly, and receiving in themselves that recompense of their error which was meet.

[28] And even as they did not like to retain God in their knowledge, God gave them over to a reprobate mind, to do those things which are not convenient."

Because the knowledge of God was corrupted, the name and identity of God was forgotten in the earth. God made plans to reveal Himself to mankind first to individuals (Abraham, Isaac, Jacob), then to a people group (Israel) and finally to the whole world, Saint John 3:16.

God planned that through various names, He would reveal the fullness of His identity. Each name would reveal something new and precious about Him. Through His names and titles, man would once again come to know the identity of God.

Below are some of the names by which He was known, and each of them revealed a little about who He is. Today looking back on what God has revealed through these names and titles, we can clearly see His identity. Follow with me and look over these scriptures and see if you get the revelation.

1. Jehovah-Jireh　　　　Provider　　　Hebrews 10:10-12
   Genesis 22:14

2. Jehovah-Rapha　　　　Healer　　　　James 5:14-15
   Exodus 15:26

3. Jehovah-Nissi　　　　Victory　　　　1 Corinthians 15:57
   Exodus 17:15

4. Jehovah-M'kaddesh　　Sanctifier　　Ephesians 5:26
   Exodus 31:13

The 10 Commandments for everyday living

5. Jehovah-Shalom   Peace   John 14:27
   Judges 6:24

6. Jehovah-Sabaoth   Lord of Hosts   James 5:4-7
   1 Samuels 1:3

7. Jehovah-Elyon   Most High   Luke 1:32, 76
   Psalms 7:17

8. Jehovah-Raah   shepherd   John 10:11
   Psalms 23:1

9. Jehovah-Hoseenu   Maker   John1:3
   Psalms 95:6

10. Jehovah-Tsidkenu Righteousness 1 Corinth 1:30
    Jeremiah 23:6

11. Jehovah-shammah   Present   Matthew 28:20
    Ezekiel 48:35

All these gifts come through the name of the Lord. ***Luke 2:11*** *"For unto you is born this day in the city of David a Saviour, which is* **Christ the Lord***"*

The name of the Lord is Jesus. The gifts above come through the name of Jesus. Jesus is Lord, so Jesus is the Lord. The Lord is God, so Jesus is God, **Deuteronomy 6:4**.

The Hebrew equivalents of the name Jesus are Joshua, Jeshua or Jeho-shua or Jehovah-shua – their meaning is, Jehovah-saves, or Jehovah-delivers.

Matthew 1:21 *"And she shall bring forth a son, and thou shalt call his name JESUS: for he shall save his people from their sins."*

It was therefore understood by Jews that Messiah would be God in the flesh born unto a virgin, *Isaiah 7:14.*

Isaiah 9:6 *"For unto us a child is born, unto us a son is given: and the government shall be upon his shoulder: and his name shall be called Wonderful, Counsellor, The mighty God, The everlasting Father, the Prince of Peace."*

Isaiah 40:3 *The voice of him that crieth in the wilderness, Prepare ye the way of the LORD, make straight in the desert a highway for our God.*
[4] Every valley shall be exalted, and every mountain and hill shall be made low: and the crooked shall be made straight, and the rough places plain:
[5] And the glory of the LORD shall be revealed, and all flesh shall see it together: for the mouth of the LORD hath spoken it.

The Jews believed Messiah would be God in the flesh. The Christians accept that Jesus is the Messiah. However there is sometimes an uncanny paradox in that some Christians do not believe that Jesus is God, and Jews generally do not accept Jesus as the Messiah.

Nevertheless Jesus is Messiah and Jesus is God. This is the revelation of the name of God. We should not take the name of Jesus in vain or treat it lightly because it's God's name.

All of the titles and names by which the Lord revealed Himself have their fulfilment in one name – JESUS. This is why Jesus is called the highest name in the Bible.

Philippians 2:9 *"Wherefore God also hath highly exalted him, and given him **a name which is above every name:***
***[10] That at the name of Jesus every knee should bow**, of things in heaven, and things in earth, and things under the earth";*

This is why there is no other name in which to receive salvation.
Acts 4:10 *"Be it known unto you all, and to all the people of Israel, that by the name of Jesus Christ of Nazareth, whom ye crucified, whom God raised from the dead, even by him doth this man stand here before you whole.*
[11] This is the stone which was set at nought of you builders, which is become the head of the corner.
*[12] Neither is there salvation in any other: **for there is none other name under heaven given among men, whereby we must be saved**."*

This is why we must do all in word or deed in the name of Jesus, ***Colossians 3:17*** *"And whatsoever ye do in word or deed, **do all in the name of the Lord Jesus**, giving thanks to God and the Father by him."*

Jesus is the fullness of the revelation of God in the New Testament age; He is quite simply God in a flesh Body,

Colossians 2:9 "*For in him dwelleth all the fulness of the Godhead bodily.*
10] And ye are complete in him, which is the head of all principality and power"

> **YOU CAN'T GET IT CLEARER THAN THAT, JESUS IS JEHOVAH.**

Not only did the Bible foretell that Jehovah would come as a man and His name is Jesus!

Isaiah 42:13 "*The LORD shall go forth as **a mighty man**, he shall stir up jealousy like a man of war: he shall cry, yea, roar; he shall prevail against his enemies.*"

The following scripture foretells that God would be the Saviour.

Isaiah 35:4 "*Say to them that are of a fearful heart, Be strong, fear not: behold, **your God will come** with vengeance, even God with a recompense; **he will come and save you.***
*[5] Then **the eyes of the blind shall be opened**, and the **ears of the deaf shall be unstopped.***
*[6] Then shall **the lame man leap** as an hart, and **the tongue of the dumb sing**: for in the wilderness shall waters break out, and streams in the desert*".

Scripture further told us how God would appear unto the world – *Isaiah 9:6 and Luke 2:11.* All of these things did come to pass that's how we know it is the truth.

Knowing this then; brings us to taking the name of the Lord in vain takes into a new dimension. The name of the Lord is the name that contains all of His characteristics, power and authority.

The name of the Lord is the name that should be respected above all other names. The name of the Lord is the name that will save us from sin. The name of the Lord is the name of the God of all the earth who is to be feared and respected above all others.

Taking the name of the Lord in vain can also mean to receive His name and be worthless e.g. or to take His name by being baptised and then to turn your back on Him by backsliding and treating His name as worthless. It also means to not live up to the high standards of behaviour expected of one who bears His name.

If you are a Christian, do you walk worthy of your calling? Or are you indifferent and careless in your Christian life?

Deuteronomy 28:58 "If thou wilt not observe to do all the words of this law that are written in this book, that thou mayest fear this glorious and fearful name, THE LORD THY GOD;"

This scripture tells us that God's glory and His name are synonymous. If we disrespect His name, we offend His glory too. To God it means the same thing.

I believe that the open disrespect of many believers for God is the main reason for much of the blasphemy of unbelievers. The sometimes-blatant hypocrisy in God's church generated by half-believers and lukewarm Christians at times stimulates the open disrespect of unbelievers for our God.

This is something that we the Church need to corporately repent of and get our example level to where it should be so that the non-believers can pattern their walk after ours without excusing their sins with our sins.

Truly when the church fears God the sinners will learn to fear God also. A good biblical example of this is the story of Ananias and Sapphira.

Acts 5:1 But a certain man named Ananias, with Sapphira his wife, sold a possession,

Acts 5:2 And kept back part of the price, his wife also being privy to it, and brought a certain part, and laid it, at the apostles' feet.

Acts 5:3 But Peter said, Ananias, why hath Satan filled thine heart to lie to the Holy Ghost, and to keep back part of the price of the land?

Acts 5:4 Whiles it remained, was it not thine own? and after it was sold, was it not in thine own power? why hast thou conceived this thing in thine heart? thou hast not lied unto men, but unto God.

Acts 5:5 And Ananias hearing these words fell down, and gave up the ghost: and great fear came on all them that heard these things.

Acts 5:6 And the young men arose, wound him up, and carried him out, and buried him.

Acts 5:7 And it was about the space of three hours after, when his wife, not knowing what was done, came in.

Acts 5:8 And Peter answered unto her, Tell me whether ye sold the land for so much? And she said, Yea, for so much.

Acts 5:9 Then Peter said unto her, How is it that ye have agreed together to tempt the Spirit of the Lord? behold, the feet of them which have buried thy husband are at the door, and shall carry thee out.

Acts 5:10 Then fell she down straightway at his feet, and yielded up the ghost: and the young men came in, and found her dead, and, carrying her forth, buried her by her husband.

Acts 5:11 And great fear came upon all the church, and upon as many as heard these things.

These kinds of wrong doing by us as Christians can do a lot of damage to the cause of Christ. The Lord only knows that many sinners use the wrong doing of 'Christians' to excuse their own sins before the Lord.

They also use it as an excuse why they do not need to live for the Lord. May the Lord help us to uphold His name and not to be guilty of causing dishonour to His name. This kind of dishonour is described as a form of blasphemy in scripture.

2 Samuel 12:13 *"And David said unto Nathan, I have sinned against the LORD. And Nathan said unto David, The LORD also hath put away thy sin; thou shalt not die.*

[14] Howbeit, because by this deed thou hast given great occasion to the enemies of the LORD to blaspheme, the child also that is born unto thee shall surely die."

Romans 2:24 *"For the name of God is blasphemed among the Gentiles through you, as it is written."*

Sinners seem to think that God condones sin, because of what they see and sometimes know to be in the lives of the saints. But God is still a Holy God, and to be respected and feared.

Preachers are sometimes guilty of preaching a God with no sense of Justice and sometimes only a God of Love. But the fear of God and the hallowing of His name go hand in hand.

> **We need to fear God and use His name with reverence. We need to preach the full original Bible plan of salvation that includes 'Repentance from Sin'.**

To be sure – blasphemers will not inherit the kingdom of heaven according to 1 Corinthians 6:9, and the book of Revelations. But read the following text.

Leviticus 24:14 "*Bring forth him that hath cursed without the camp; and let all that heard him lay their hands upon his head, and let all the congregation stone him.*
[15] And thou shalt speak unto the children of Israel, saying, Whosoever curseth his God shall bear his sin.
[16] And he that blasphemeth the name of the LORD, he shall surely be put to death, and all the congregation shall certainly stone him: as well the stranger, as he that is born in the land, when he blasphemeth the name of the LORD, shall be put to death"

2Timothy 3:1-5 also tells us that God's Word is against all profanity. Humans were never meant to take the name of the Lord their God in vain.

This basically means more than just saying the name without any significance as in the way some use the name of Jesus as a curse word for when they strike their toe on the ground or some other trivial matter.

To take the Lord's name in vain can be to misuse His name and abuse it; by saying, "I will do all these things in His name." Then proceed not to do it.

James 4:17 "*Therefore to him that knoweth to do good, and doeth it not, to him it is sin*"

Better it would be if you simply did not do what you said you would do; even that you had the intent and did not say, and did not do; than that you should swear in the name of the Lord and not do what you said under oath. It means to treat His name as though it were nothing.

To deny God's name the regal treatment it deserves, with its rights, respect and honour is blasphemy. It means to look upon using His name lightly, in the sense of jokingly.

It means to make His name out to be like it was any other ordinary name. God is saying, *"You do not do that to My name. My name is holy, you treat it with respect."*

> **Respect Is Due To Jesus Because Jesus Is God and His Name Is Holy.** It often isn't difficult to persuade people in general that the name of Jesus is special, but getting them to see that the name of Jesus is the name of God is the key to revelation about the importance of that name – Jesus is God and therefore the name of Jesus is the name of God.

CHAPTER 4

The law of rest explained as rest – Law number 4

Exodus 20:8 "*Remember the sabbath day, to keep it holy.*
[9] Six days shalt thou labour, and do all thy work:
[10] But the seventh day is the sabbath of the LORD thy God: in it thou shalt not do any work, thou, nor thy son, nor thy daughter, thy manservant, nor thy maidservant, nor thy cattle, nor thy stranger that is within thy gates:
[11] For in six days the LORD made heaven and earth, the sea, and all that in them is, and rested the seventh day: wherefore the LORD blessed the sabbath day, and hallowed it."

Enough to say the seventh day was the identifying mark of the covenant called the Law. This agreement was made between God, Moses and Israel. No other nation or people were included in this covenant as we shall see later.

When they remembered that day, they would automatically remember that covenant, through this memorial; they were identifying themselves with each other as a group party to the blessings and curses that were the rightful inheritance of the covenant keeper or the covenant breaker.

The only way at that time to be party to that covenant was to become an Israelite by circumcision (initiation) and keep the Law. With the keeping of the seventh day the seal of the covenant was confirmed in the life of every individual. It was the ever present sign of the covenant of the law.

The Sabbath was the mark that distinguished this covenant from every other covenant God had made with mankind or any individual. The word Sabbath meant rest. It meant to stop working and to start resting.

All this and more is foundational to when God said to Israel, "Remember the Sabbath day", keep this in mind. I will come back to this in a little while and exposit it in more depth than the rest of the other commandments.

I believe this commandment requires some special attention; but after He said to remember the Sabbath day, He continued so follow me to the next thought and see if this makes sense?

> **Rest is made for man to rest so when it's time to rest, what we need is not an extra job, part-time or overtime, but rest means exactly that! Stop working and or cease all labouring activity. You can't side-step it Sabbath means – rest!**

Let's Talk Sabbath
How does all this begin to fit together? What happened to the law? Did anything happen to the law indeed? What was supposed to be the meaning of the Sabbath in the New Testament?

Matthew 5: 17-18 'Till heaven and earth pass away not one jot nor one tittle shall in no wise pass from the law till all be fulfilled.'

Did He say that the law would not pass away? No. Did He say that the law would not be abolished, the answer is no. Did He say that the law would always be there the answer is no.

He said that it would not pass away until it was fulfilled. In other words it would remain until it had served its purpose. The law has a purpose and would not be removed until it was fulfilled.

The Ten Commandments are not all of the law, but they are symbolic of the total content of the law. They point to the relationship between God and man and the relationship between man and man. They deal with every aspect of our life and expand out to 613 precepts.

In these 613 precepts outlined and explained throughout the Torah (first five books of the Bible) God does not leave any aspect unturned.

He deals with everything you can think of even down to how to go to the toilet. But, there is a reason why the Sabbath was given special attention by God and it had a prominence that entitles it to special treatment in this work.

It is because I believe that this subject is very important that this book is called "Let's talk Sabbath" it was important and is important today that we fully understand this subject.

The Introduction to the Sabbath
The Sabbath was quite simply a day given as the sealing sign or token of the Old Testament Commandments. There was one sign or token of the covenant, which was given to the people before the law, which is the sign of circumcision.

With the law came the institution of the Sabbath, so the Sabbath is the key precept of the institution of the law.

As long as the law stands the Sabbath stands. When the law is abolished the Sabbath too is abolished. Now I know that you may not agree with this, but why don't we just simply agree to allow the scripture to speak and prove all things.

I am trying to show that if you read **Exodus Chapter 20** there were more than just Ten Commandments given. In fact what happened meant that God had to stop audibly speaking to all the people after he said those first Ten Commandments.

He then said no more in an audible voice that all of them could hear, because the people were afraid. But He continued through Moses.

Moses went closer to where God was, and communed with God. God actually gave another 45 commandments while Moses was on that mountain.

But, the first ten were the only commandments of the law that God gave that all could hear. They all heard the voice of God. However no one saw a form or shape.

After this manifestation, they couldn't say God had never spoken to them. Many today challenge us as Christians by saying,"If God spoke to me then I would give my life to Him immediately".

This kind of statement is tempting God. God speaks to us today through His word and through His servants; because He has already made a point that man cannot bear it if He would speak to us directly.

The Fourth Commandment - Sabbath

Now the fourth commandment said, *"Remember the Sabbath day"*, so they must have had an understanding of what God meant when he said remember the Sabbath day.

The meaning of the word SABBATH comes from the Hebrew word Shabbath which means to rest (this is the primary meaning – rest) it also means to sever, desist, to come to an end, an intermission.

It means to take a break. In the Assyrian language it meant the rest of the heart or peace of mind. So then rest means Sabbath and Sabbath means rest. The words are interchangeable in scripture and this is the principal thing we must establish at the onset.

The first mention of rest or Sabbath in connection with the seventh day is found in *Genesis 2:1-3*. God had created all things including man in six days, and God then rested or desisted from His work of creating.

God rested or sabbathed on the seventh day and blessed and sanctified that day. At this point I would like to make it clear that God does not stipulate this to be a law or commandment here in Genesis.

Now you're going to hear some funny people say, Oh! God got tired so God rested. Our God doesn't slumber nor sleep; our God doesn't get tired. God is seeking to speak in a way that we can understand. When the Bible says that God rested it means that He stopped all creative work.

He stopped creating, and on the seventh day He did no more creating. In the like manner, as God created for six days and on the seventh rested, they were to work for six days and on the seventh day they were to rest.

"This is my time between me (Jehovah) and the children of Israel." Amen.

God does however establish a principle of one day's rest in seven. He knew a man could not work non-stop without need to take a break.

God knew a seven-day cycle was necessary. Six days work and one day rest is necessary. Anyone trying to go against this principle will suffer the consequence in his or her health.

Notice from this particular portion of scripture, that the Bible specifically outlines that in the beginning God laid down a pattern that there would be six days of work and there would be one day of rest.

This is because no one and nothing can ever continue to burn the midnight oil at both ends and when it meets in the middle still be strong. This is the consequence in your health that I spoke of early. You'll get sick if you don't let your body have regular rest.

Regular to God means you must rest at least one day in seven. We all know that if you work seven days a week you feel so tired and so drained but just one day can make a real and definite difference.

So, that's why God put in a principle of rest from the very beginning, but no where in Genesis does He order anyone to keep it. He just outlines that this is what he did and the Bible leaves it at that.

So we can boldly say God did not give command concerning the keeping of a Sabbath by man in Genesis. It was not made a law at that time and anyone who says different is simply not being true to scripture or to themselves. To find out what God would do with the principle of rest established in Genesis, we must go further into the Bible.

The next mention of Sabbath

Well if you turn to Exodus Chapter 16 you will see where the Sabbath day was first mentioned in connection with any commandment or law. Here God gave bread from Heaven and he told the people to gather. *Exodus 16 verse 22-30* says:

Exodus 16:22 And it came to pass, that on the sixth day they gathered twice as much bread, two omers for one man: and all the rulers of the congregation came and told Moses.

Exodus 16:23 And he said unto them, This is that which the LORD hath said, Tomorrow is the rest of the holy Sabbath unto the LORD: bake that which ye will bake to day, and seethe that ye will seethe; and that which remaineth over lay up for you to be kept until the morning.

Exodus 16:24 And they laid it up till the morning, as Moses bade: and it did not stink, neither was there any worm therein.

Exodus 16:25 And Moses said, Eat that to day; for to day is a sabbath unto the LORD: to day ye shall not find it in the field.

Exodus 16:26 Six days ye shall gather it; but on the seventh day, which is the sabbath, in it there shall be none.

Exodus 16:27 And it came to pass, that there went out some of the people on the seventh day for to gather, and they found none.

Exodus 16:28 And the LORD said unto Moses, How long refuse ye to keep my commandments and my laws?

Exodus 16:29 See, for that the LORD hath given you the sabbath, therefore he giveth you on the sixth day the bread of two days; abide ye every man in his place, let no man go out of his place on the seventh day.

Exodus 16:30 So the people rested on the seventh day.

For six days manna fell in the camp of Israel, with twice as much falling on the Sixth day of the week. This gave them all sufficient food for the seventh day, as no manna fell on that day. Israel was clearly instructed not even to go out of their dwelling on the seventh day.

It was to be one day wholly dedicated to God alone. Those who observed a Sabbath day kept this ruling. They did no work, no cooking, and no travelling and did not even leave their house if they were really serious Jews.

The first time ever that God commanded man to rest on a particular day is found right here in *Exodus Chapter 16*. It was not a command from the time that God did his creative acts in Genesis. It was from *Exodus Chapter 16* when God gave out the manna.

Here He told them that from then on the seventh day would be for rest. This is because that is what Sabbath means, it means to rest. As the Bible says they couldn't come out of their homes they just had to stay in their house and rest.

No work just rest. So in the Commandments that's why it says remember the Sabbath day and keep it holy, for it was to be one day fully set aside to be with the Lord God.

Exodus 23:12 Six days thou shalt do thy work, and **on the seventh day thou shalt rest**: that thine ox and thine ass may rest, and the son of thy handmaid, and the stranger, may be refreshed.

The Sabbath Made Very Clear - Written
What we have discovered so far is that God, from *Exodus Chapter 20* straight through to *Exodus Chapter 24* was giving quite a few different commandments but the first ten were the only ones that He spoke to the people with his voice. After that the people let Moses become their representative before God.

Jesus the Messiah, who knows best the application of scripture, allowed His disciples to pluck corn on the Sabbath day, thus apparently breaking the Law of Moses according to the Jews. His answer was that the Sabbath was made for man and not man for the Sabbath.

Matthew 12:1-8, Mark 2:23-26, Luke 6:1-10. This same Jesus healed on the Sabbath day and the Jew accused Him of being a Sabbath breaker. *John 5:1-18, Luke 13:10-17.*

Once did Jesus indicate or tell anyone to observe a certain day for a Sabbath in all of His teachings to the people. Surely if it was a salvation issue would He not have given this teaching a place of prominence. Instead we find Him stressing the importance of the attitudes of the heart toward God.

If Jesus had intended for mankind in the New Testament period to keep the Sabbath, why didn't He mention it? Not even in His requirements to the rich young ruler to whom He showed that covetousness was in his heart **Matthew 19:16-22**.

Jesus left no indication of the Sabbath's supposed importance, but He did teach that the law was fulfilled when we love God and our neighbour as ourselves, not when we observe a day **Matthew 22:34-40, Galatians 5:14, James 2:8**.

So it's not a case of we keep one of the laws or five or we keep nine, we must fulfil all of the law. In **Acts 15:5, 7-11, 28, 29** certain brethren troubled the gentiles (non-Jews) by teaching them that they were still under the old covenant. The question required the gathering of the first Apostolic Council with the express purpose of settling this matter once and for all.

We are dealing with Sabbath in the context of the Law **Acts 15: 5 and 19-21**. Notice that this particular occasion was the occasion where the law was being put on trial. Is the law for the gentiles? The had a great big elders counsel where they all sat down and discussed and debated whether or not everyone should not keep the law.

Whether or not everyone was not bound by the precepts of the law and should they not honour the law by being circumcised (which makes them a Jew) and by keeping the law which secondly makes them part of the Old Covenant.

The answer was these things were too heavy to bear by our forefathers and we ourselves couldn't keep them. So why should we put such a burden on the Gentiles. Therefore it seems good to us and to the Holy Ghost not just to themselves.

So they began to say that these are the things that we consider necessary for the Gentiles to be able to make it into heaven; they need to stop fornicating, stop blood sacrifices and drinking blood, they need to stop eating dead things.

Dead things have their blood in them, they need to honour these particular precepts and by so doing they will make it if they live out the rest of the faith of grace. God's Holy Spirit in other words, would teach them what they had to do.

The summary is that neither they nor their forefathers were able to keep the law (that includes the Sabbath) so it is unreasonable to expect the gentiles to do so.

They went on to establish certain necessary things. They pointed out that they were all saved through God purifying their hearts by faith, through the grace of the Lord Jesus Christ.

No decision is recorded here regarding us keeping the Sabbath though it would have been a good place to record it if it was required. The only possible conclusion must be that it wasn't one of "the necessary things" they agreed upon. It isn't even mentioned. Doesn't that strike you as strange?

Paul, who was in attendance at the council of Jerusalem, was a Pharisee and was trained to observe the Old Testament Sabbath *Acts 13:42, 16:13* also see *Acts 18:14*.

Strangely however in all his writings (approx. two thirds of the new testament.) he never once indicated that New Testament believers are to observe a day as a Sabbath.

In fact he was instrumental in taking the dispute about the law to the Apostolic Council in Jerusalem where they decided what was necessary and what was not, *Acts 15*.

Paul in His writings gives liberty in esteeming any day as unto the Lord. Why that's because the issue isn't a day but a covenant.

He says it's not important what you eat or don't eat as long as you do it unto the Lord, *Romans 14:5-6*. He neither demands nor suggests the observance of a certain day unto the Lord. In this matter we have liberty.

He is quite clear that the Sabbath of the Law of Moses was a schoolmaster and shadow of things to come. *Colossians 2:16-17* and *Galatians 3:10, 24-25*. In *Galatians 4:9-11*, Paul warned the Galatians church on the matter of observing days, months, times and years.

Galatians 3:24-29 Points out that the children of promise (Christians) are not under the old covenant or schoolmaster, which would hold us in bondage, but we are under Christ, *Galatians 5:1*

> **We can find the laws of the new covenant very easily, they are in the Epistles, and are called the laws of Christ.**

In 1 Corinthians 9:20-21, Paul explains that though he was not in bondage to the old covenant, he was not without law. He was now under the law of Christ.

Most probably the person who is speaking to you or asking you that question about, "what are you doing about the Sabbath?" Is not born again, by being baptised in Jesus' name, and has not got the Holy Spirit abiding in them.

Lets Talk Sabbath some more

Then the Bible goes on to say that God drove us in and we drive in him. Jesus Christ is our abiding place; we rest in him. If you want to talk about Sabbath or rest the true meaning of the new covenant rest is that we rest from our work.

When scripture said I will give you rest, the word rest means I will give you an abode, a resting-place, I will give you a place where you can lay down.

When the Bible speaks of a better rest in the book of Hebrews, then what it is referring to is found in *Isaiah 28* as prophesied by God through Isaiah. There God says," *with another tongue and stammering lips will I speak unto the people since this is the rest where we shall rest, this is the refreshing."*

Under the old covenant the Bible says you cease from working you don't work; what was our work, back then it was physical. Today under the New Testament, the works we cease from are our own dead works of sin.

The Bible calls them works of unrighteousness. So when God calls you to salvation, God is saying cease from your work and I have some good works, which I have ordained before the foundation of the world that you should walk into them.

A good explanation of the person who has ceased from their own works and has entered into true Sabbath is found in *Titus 3:5*. We enter into rest by the renewing of the Holy Ghost. It is not you that live, but Christ lives and works in you. You are at rest, you have ceased from your works and God is working in and through you.

We are His workmanship, so when you repented of your sins and was baptised in Jesus' name and received God's Spirit you ceased from your works; you no longer live unto yourself, you now live unto God.

For you to now turn round and say well I want to do my will, I want to do my own thing is the same as the man who picked up sticks *Numbers chapter 35* and gathered them to burn on the Sabbath day because he went against the clearly revealed will of God.

God is telling us that in Christ Jesus we remain in rest. The rest of, the Holy Spirit. I live in you, "now that's why he says take my yolk its easy.

Because He will live in you don't act as you like by doing anything you want; I live in you; I live my life through you; I fulfil my righteousness in you; I work to my will what my good pleasure is through you.

Exodus 31:15 Six days may work be done; but in the seventh is the sabbath of rest, holy to the LORD: whosoever doeth any work in the sabbath day, he shall surely be put to death.
Exodus 31:16 Wherefore the children of Israel shall keep the sabbath, to observe the sabbath throughout their generations, for a perpetual covenant.

Exodus 31:17 It is a sign between me and the children of Israel for ever: for in six days the LORD made heaven and earth, and on the seventh day he rested, and was refreshed.

Exodus 31:18 And he gave unto Moses, when he had made an end of communing with him upon mount Sinai, two tables of testimony, tables of stone, written with the finger of God.

Whom did God make that covenant with? God made that covenant with the children of Israel. What was the sign then of that covenant? The Sabbath day that's what it says.

Let's Look Briefly At Some Scriptural Requirements Of Sabbath Keeping In The Scripture.

Any person not found to be keeping the Sabbath was to be put to death. In *Exodus 35:2* God says this plainly.

Later on in scripture, a certain man was stoned to death because that on the Sabbath he was found picking up sticks. This to God constituted breaking the Sabbath commandment in *Numbers 15:32-36.*

Every seventh year was a sabbatical year, when Israel did not plant any crops, it was the Sabbath of the land *Leviticus 25:3-7. Exodus 23:10-11.*

No work was to be done on the seventh day itself. Some today would say that although they do shift work so God understand, yet others would say that what they do falls into the category of missions of mercy, e.g. nursing.

I wonder how Moses would have seen these excuses? Now I want to be clear here, I am not seeking to judge anyone, I am merely examining things from the perspective of the Law.

Some people say that they do not break the Sabbath. They consider their work to be works of mercy, just like Jesus said, 'you could pull out a sheep out of a pit on the Sabbath day'. Why shouldn't I work because I am doing it as a work of mercy or shift work or part-time work?

The fact is for most people it is their job. It is not a work of mercy like an incidental helping out of someone who needs help, but rather it is a daily or weekly breaking of such a commandment as was given. And if indeed that commandment was still in force today there is one thing that would happen to them, they would all be stoned.

Numbers 15:32 And while the children of Israel were in the wilderness, they found a man that gathered sticks upon the sabbath day.
Numbers 15:33 And they that found him gathering sticks brought him unto Moses and Aaron, and unto all the congregation.
Numbers 15:34 And they put him in ward, because it was not declared what should be done to him.
Numbers 15:35 And the LORD said unto Moses, The man shall be surely put to death: all the congregation shall stone him with stones without the camp.

Numbers 15:36 *And all the congregation brought him without the camp, and stoned him with stones, and he died; as the LORD commanded Moses*

In the book of Numbers we find a certain man who went out to gather some sticks for a fire on the Sabbath day and God was asked by Moses what shall we do with him for they had put him inward (imprisoned) temporarily till they should know the will of God. Knowing the will of God is one of the most important things that we can do.

So then when Moses found out that the will of God was to stone this man they stoned him and they heaped stones upon him.

Why? Because he had gone out and worked on the Sabbath day. We thank God that we are not under the law, but are under grace or we would be implementing some big time stoning.

No one else was to work on the Sabbath either. Well some say, 'how about getting someone else who does not believe as you do to take your place?'

Didn't the law forbid your ox, manservant or male-servant to do work too? Well into what category does the unbeliever a slave to sin fall? How would Moses interpret you getting someone else to do for you what should not be done according to the Law?

It seems to me that Moses may not have been very happy with some of the interpretations that many modern day practitioners of the law seek to apply to it? The choice appears to be either you keep it all or not at all.
This is James' advice, **James 2:10,** "For whosoever shall keep the whole law, and yet offend in one point, he is guilty of all".

James' advice amounts to this, 'don't even try to keep the law because you are bound to fail, and when you fail in one point the reward for failing to keep the whole Law is yours'. The reward for failure to satisfy the demands of the Law is death.

Every seven times seven years was a special Sabbath year called the Jubilee *Leviticus 25:8-11.*

Israel was commanded not to kindle a fire on the Sabbath day, *Exodus 35:3* that mean no cooking or even lighting one to stay warm.

These rules applied exclusively to the Sabbaths of Israel. If you observe a Sabbath, do you keep any or all of these rules? For the law and the Sabbath are all linked together in total unity as one, they are one and the same.

The New Testament Sabbath

What is the sign today that God has sanctified us? The in-filling of the Holy Ghost. So the sign of the New Testament is not the Sabbath but it's the seal of the Holy Ghost. And the sign of the Holy Ghost in-filling is speaking in other tongues *Exodus 31: 12-14.*

Never in any other generation have people spoken in tongues until the day of Pentecost in 33A.D. Never in any other generation have people been filled with the Holy Ghost as we, but yet people where filling with the Holy Ghost before the New Testament however, not speaking in other tongues. Speaking in other tongues is a sign or seal of the New Testament Covenant, which God has enjoined to His people.

The New Testament law is not written on stone but the heart, it's not written by man, but by the spirit of the Lord. The secret of liberty from the law is that you must have the Holy Ghost.

When you have the Holy Ghost you are freed from the law. The law is abolished to you and you to the law. The law is dead to you and you to the law. Until such a time the law will convict of sin, or righteousness and of judgement.
2 Corinthians 3: 3

If there had been a law given which could have given lift verily righteousness should have been by the law. Righteousness could not be by the law, but, if the law is all that was necessary then God could have made us righteous through it.

So something else was necessary. The law was our teacher to show us that we needed a saviour. The law was as our instructor to show us that Jesus is an absolute necessity to our life if we are to stop sinning **Galatians 3: 21-26**.

The law was our instructor to show us we cannot live our life on our own terms accepting we want to be destroyed. The law is our teacher to show us that without God we cannot make it. We no longer have to walk with the mind of the Ten Commandments.

We no longer have to walk trying to keep the Sabbath day. We no longer have to be mindful of these things because now we are under a higher standard. We are under the New Testament. You are not the children of God by keeping the law but by Jesus Christ.

These people had been freed from the law and now someone had come in and told them it was important to keep the law and He says how return you again to the weak and beggarly elements of the law *Galatians 4: 9-10*.

The law is not strong, the law is weak, and the law is not going to help you into heaven it is going to hinder you from getting into heaven.

Its purpose is to reveal and to show sin to reveal and to show Christ. Christ is the end of the law. The law leads you to Christ and once you have found Christ why return to the weak and beggarly elements.

In *Colossians 2:16, 17*, Paul opens up the revelation concerning meats (food) and Sabbath. They are, he says, a type and shadow of something that is to come.

This scripture goes on to teach that Christ is the substance, behind every shadow and type of the Old Testament. Remember that; behind every shadow is a substance. Therefore the command to keep the shadow (Sabbath) is fulfilled in the substance (Jesus).

The substance – Jesus is the one who gives the true meaning to Sabbath. Remember I told you that Sabbath means rest? Well listen to this, "come unto me all ye who labour and are heavy laden and I will give you rest (Sabbath)." That was spoken by Jesus in *Matthew 11:28.*

In **Hebrews 4:8-11** Scripture records that under Joshua, Israel did not have the rest of God in their souls, Though they kept the physical day, but they were told of another day (The day of grace and salvation), when the rest of God would fill the hearts of believers. That's the Holy Ghost.

In **Exodus 31:13-15**, we found the Sabbath was a sign or seal between God and His covenant people (The children of Israel). We find that it was given to them as the sign of that covenant that they might know Him as the rest (Sabbath) of Israel.

In like manner, in a similar way God's New Testament covenant people (Christians) were given the seal of the Holy Ghost as the sign of the New Testament covenant that they might know Jesus as Lord and be sanctified. The Holy Ghost is the seal of the New Testament covenant between God and His people today. ***Ephesians 1:13, 14; Ephesians 4:30; 1Corinthians 12:3; 1 Corinthians 1:30.***

In **Exodus 31:14, 15** the penalty for breaking the Sabbath rest was death. And in the New Testament the penalty is still death if we break our covenantal relationship. It is spiritual death to break the seal of God by blaspheming the Holy Ghost out of your life.

It is spiritual death to continue in your own dead work rather than rely upon God's grace. It is spiritual death to so harden your heart against the clear witness of the Holy Ghost that God cannot convict your heart. It is spiritual death to sin and not repent, **Romans 6:23.**

After looking at **Colossians 2: 16,** the question we must ask is this, "Is the Sabbath a holy day"? Yes. It is a holy day which has been separated by God but let no man judge you about these things because Jesus Christ is the end of the seventh day Sabbath.

What is a shadow? Is the sun casting light upon you the reality or the shadow? Who is the real thing, Jesus Christ! He is the embodiment of all of these things. He is the reality of all of these things.

He is the end of all of these things. So the Sabbath has its fulfilment in Christ Jesus. The bulls and goats being killed have their fulfilment in Jesus. The altar the door of the tabernacle, the Brazen altar and brazen laver every single aspect of the tabernacle has its fulfilment in Jesus.

Every law that was given has its fulfilment in Jesus. Everything that happened in the Old Testament that showed the righteous anger of God and the mercy of God have their fulfilment in Jesus. Jesus is the fulfilment of all the shadows that are in the Old Testament.

In other words the law is there to expose sin. That's its purpose. If the preacher preaches about sin he must use the law and if he uses the law people will be convicted. People will be convinced of their need to return to Christ, **1 Timothy 1: 5, 8-11.**

But in returning to Christ we find mercy and we find grace available. By grace are you saved, through faith not of yourselves it's a gift of God lest any man should boast.

Boast of what? boast of your good works of how you have achieved all this, how you have kept the law, how you have kept the Sabbath day and you have done all manner of things that make you worthy of going to heaven.

No man is ever worthy of going to heaven for heaven is by grace. If it be by grace then it's not by works and if it be by works then it's not by faith but yet there is a middle ground through which works and faith combine.

In Hebrews God begins to open up the understanding that we have a better covenant in the New Testament. It is better bar far and exceeds with light years between them, *Hebrews 7: 19.*

There is no comparison between the two covenants. They are not just simply better but exceedingly better. We have a better covenant in the New Testament. The New Testament is the better hope and it is through that that we draw near to God *(Verse 22).*

This is the payment for that testament, *Hebrews 8: 7, 10 and 13.* Indeed many aspects of the old have been included in the new but the old one is there simply for information and the new one is there for you to live out.

Hebrews 9: 15-18 and 22. Jesus said preach repentance and remission of sins in my name. In his name the New Testament blood is sprinkled or applied to people's lives. In his name the bible says you find life.

These things are written that you may believe that Jesus Christ is the Son of God and that believing you might have life though His name. In other words the blood is sprinkled or applied to our life through His name.

His name is that which sprinkles and applies the New Testament to you and makes you a part of the New Covenant just as in the Old Testament the blood would be sprinkled with the hyssop upon the people and as they were sprinkled they expected that they were joined to the Old Covenant. Today you are joined to the new through Jesus Christ.

By a new and living way which He has consecrated for us through the veil that is to say his flesh. Through his sacrifice we have been joined to that New Testament, **Hebrews 10: 20.**

If you try to keep the law and miss one of the 613 precepts you are guilty of everything. Isn't it better to just try and keep the one, **James 2: 2-20.** You can love your neighbour as yourself and do well **(Verse 11)**.

Even so faith without works is dead being alone. Dead faith is the kind which believes nothing but the kind of faith that God is looking for the kind that fulfils the law is the kind that says I believe in God and I will obey Him.

I will follow Him wheresoever he leads me. I will do what he instructs me in my heart to do for you see the law is no longer external but it is internalised.

Its in your heart by the holy spirit and the spirit that is in you will bid you come, will bid you go, will bid you this is the right way walk though in it and when He tells you it and you do it you walk about the physical law.

You walk above the law that is written in letter because you don't need the letters to remind you to follow him. The law is abolished to everyone that is in Christ Jesus. To everyone that is drawn by is spirit. You will instead have a rest of faith in Christ Jesus. We simply trust in Jesus.

That is the true meaning of this rest – Jesus. The only way a man cannot enter into this rest which is on offer to all the world is told us in the book of **Hebrews chapter 4** it says, that its through disobedience and unbelief that we are hindered from having access.

Then the writer tells us by the Holy Ghost to beware lest like the children of Israel who failed to possess the Promised Land, that God does not have to swear that you won't enter into that rest.

Can you imagine God was fighting for them and supplying their every need? But when it came to possessing the Promised Land by faith in God who worked for Israel, the failed, because they looked at things only from their own points of view.

Only two men from that generation were able to enter in, Joshua and Caleb, men of faith, men who took God at His word and relied upon Him for the fulfilment of His promises.

> **Let us labour therefore that we enter into this rest, how? Simply by being obedient to God.**

So then it is through the new covenant that God puts the spirit of the law in our hearts, and He places the righteousness of the law on our undeserving account. By declaring us righteous. Through nothing we have done, we have entered into relationship through cutting covenant with Jesus alone.

So we don't serve God because we have to we serve God because we love to. Love is the fulfilling of the law so you fulfil every commandment of God through love; all of them.

That's why the Bible says if there is any other commandment it is fulfilled through your love, **Romans 13:8-10**. If you keep it you fulfil the entire commandment, *1 John 3:23, 24.*

From what we have studied, it should have become clear that the old covenant that God made with Israel has been set aside for the New Testament He has made with the church. The new covenant or testament is a part of a spiritual kingdom founded upon the law of the spirit of life in Christ Jesus *Romans 8:2*.

Because Jesus Christ is the end or fulfilment of the law of righteousness (judgement) to believers Romans 10:4, when we believe, we are seal with the Holy Ghost and so enter into rest. The Sabbath of the Holy Ghost where our works cease and God's work in us continues, *Ephesians 1:3, 14; Isaiah 29:11, 12.*

There is also coming a day (a time period in the future) when God will give rest to all creation. All creation will enjoy Sabbath. *Isaiah 11:6-11* speaks of God's rest in this time when the whole earth will be at rest. And again in *Isaiah 14:3-7*.

1. It becomes clear that God could not rest and will not rest while the whole earth is filled with pain, sorrow, and death, *John 5:17* "*My father worketh.*"

2. In the day of God's rest sorrow and sighing shall flee away, for the knowledge of the Lord shall cover the earth as the waters cover the sea *Isaiah 35:10*.

3. The bottom line concerning a physical Sabbath day in the New Testament church from its commencement till now is this; such a day does not exist scripturally.

4. From the day of Pentecost, there is no record of any Christian ever keeping the first or the seventh day as a Sabbath to keep a law that pleases God.

5. Sabbath is not a day but a person, Sabbath is Jesus. Accept Him and you will find *rest for your soul*. For only He can give you that peace which passes all understanding.

The Conclusion of the Matter of Sabbath

We have established that we should not even try to keep the 10 Commandments. We cannot keep them, but through faith in Christ we can fulfil them. In trying to keep the Law, we fall from grace and frustrate God's plan to save us.

We must therefore fulfil God's plan through the establishment of the New Covenant in our own personal life. What was an historic event must become a personal experience for each of us individually. This happens when:

1. When we believe on the Name of the Lord Jesus Christ and love our neighbour as ourself. Through this we fulfil the whole Ten Commandments that pertain to God and to man – *1 John 3:23-24; Romans 13:8-10.*

2. When we believe on Jesus Christ for our justification and the remission of our sins, we establish the second covenant and fulfil the ten commandments - **Romans 3:31, Acts 2:38-39**.

3. When we enter into Christ Jesus and abide in the Law of His Spirit, the righteousness of the Ten Commandments is fulfilled in us - **Galatians 3:27; Romans 8:4.**

4. When we believe on Christ Jesus as Saviour, we may live in His liberty, knowing that Christ is the end of the 10 Commandments. Through this we establish the New Covenant in our lives - **Romans 10:4; 2 Corinthians 3:17**.

5. When we commit fully to Christ's authority over our life and submit to His will, we have then ceased from our works, and now do the works which God, has ordained for us, knowing that it is God that works in us, ***Ephesians 2:10; Philippians 2:13; Hebrews 13:21.***

Through this we are labouring to enter into the eternal rest that remains for the people of God, ***Hebrews 4:9-11.***

Those who refuse to remain in the liberty of the New Covenant and the justification that comes by faith alone in Christ Jesus through obedience of the New Testament original plan of salvation are returning like a piglet to its mire and like a dog to its vomit.

They return to something the Bible calls bondage in trying to keep the Old Testament in part or in full. Seeking to be justified by it, the scripture plainly states in making the following four points that:

1. You have fallen from grace - *Galatians 5:4*

2. You frustrate the Grace of God - *Galatians 2:21*

3. Christ's death upon the cross was in vain for you. This makes the gospel of Christ pointless to you and lightly esteemed by you - *Galatians 2:21*.
4. You are in bondage - *Galatians 4:9-11*

To all those who read this book, I encourage you in the Grace of God, and by the Name of our Lord and Saviour Jesus Christ.

Cut covenant with Jesus through His name by repenting of your sins and being baptised in the Name of our Lord Jesus Christ and be sealed with the baptism of the Holy Ghost speaking in other tongues as God gives you the utterance - *Acts 2:38; Ephesians 1:13.*

Thereafter walk in the Grace of God steadfastly and stand firmly in the liberty wherewith /Christ hat made you free, and be not entangled with the yoke of bondage that comes through seeking to keep rather than fulfil the Law - *Galatians 5:1*. May God richly bless you as we proceed further in the the mystery of the Law.

A new thing for Israel is that god will make a new covenant with them. (this will mean the old one must be gone and cease to be in force from that time forward).

A new thing for the gentiles – we get a part in the new Covenant through the messiah

CHAPTER 5

The law of respect explained as the law of honour – Law number 5

Exodus 20:12 "Honor thy father and thy mother: that thy days may be long upon the land which the LORD thy God giveth thee."

This then is the law God spoke against parental dishonour. I believe that God gave this commandment knowing that if we were to be allowed to dishonour our earthly parents unchallenged, then we would also dishonour our heavenly parent too.

Here God makes it clear that we ought to honour our father and our mother. Many people today honour either father or mother, but God requires us to honour them both. Others still respect neither father nor mother. Some go further and actually hate their father and mother. This is a sin that needs to be repented of.

Be careful here, for in the New Testament, God reaffirms this command and links it to long life, **Matthew 15:4** *"For God commanded, saying, Honour thy father and mother: and, He that curseth father or mother, let him die the death."*

Ephesians 6:2 *"Honour thy father and mother; which is the first commandment with promise;*

Ephesians 6:3 *That it may be well with thee, and thou mayest live long on the earth." The implications here are clear. We should honour our parents because God commanded it, and it will lengthen our lives"*

The promise from God is a long life for those who honour their parents and a shortened one for those who dishonour their parents. This makes a shortened life a curse.

This command is about family life. Honour speaks primarily of respect, but includes affection, gratitude, love and obedience. If there was ever a day when children were ungrateful to their parents, this is that day?

If ever there was a time when children have no respect, or affection for their parents, it's today? In our day children are disobedient and dishonouring to their parents by the vanload. God said we must honour our parents.

I believe God is expecting us to teach our children by our examples how they too should honour their parents in due time by how we treat ours today.

The Bible gives us only one glimpse of Jesus: childhood, and in it we are told that he subjected himself to his parents. **Luke 2:51.**

During His public ministry Jesus condemned the Pharisees for evading their child to parent responsibilities using excuses.

Matthew 15:3 "But he answered and said unto them, Why do ye also transgress the commandment of God by your tradition?
[4] For God commanded, saying, Honour thy father and mother: and, He that curseth father or mother, let him die the death.
[5] But ye say, Whosoever shall say to his father or his mother, It is a gift, by whatsoever thou mightest be profited by me;

Matthew 15:6 *And honour not his father or his mother, he shall be free. Thus have ye made the commandment of God of none effect by your tradition".*

At His crucifixion, in the midst of agony He remembered and had time to delegate His responsibility to look after His mother to John the beloved disciple, ***John 19:27.***
One Biblical sign of the last days is disobedience to parent's, ***2Timothy 3:1-5.***

As long as our parents live we have the opportunity and responsibility to care for them.

Timothy I 5:8 *"But if any provide not for his own, and specially for those of his own house (family), he hath denied the faith, and is worse than an infidel."*

Proverbs 30:17 *"The eye that mocketh at his father, and despiseth to obey his mother, the ravens of the valley shall pick it out, and the young eagles shall eat it."*

The truth of the matter is that there are some reading this book that still have unsettled scores of hatred, resentment, hurts, and unforgiveness toward their parents. Of course I don't mean you?

It must be one of the others that are reading this book. There are also those of you who are just plain ungrateful and feel no obligation or responsibility toward your parents.

You're wrong to entertain such thoughts, and God is watching you He is observing your heart to see what you will do. We should all remember that our example is also planting seeds, which we will reap through your own children. What we do to our parents will come back to us.

Our children are watching our example, they learn more by what we do than by what we say. What they will remember about us, will be the things they saw acted out most frequently in front of their eyes. Ask yourself what do you want them to remember? Are you doing what you want them to remember about you?

Honouring our father and mother is unconditional. I hear someone saying, "but you don't know what that man/woman did to me!" Honouring them is still unconditional.

Whether they are worthy or unworthy, fair or foul, the issue is honour. The crunch is respect. You are required to be obedient to the commandment.

Respect your parents. Esau disrespected his father by marrying Gentile wives. In *Genesis 26:35*; Ham the son of Noah disrespected his father by looking upon his nakedness to the cursing of his son's lineage. Have you disrespected your parents in any way you can think of? Seek to right it as soon as possible.

Leviticus 19:3 Ye shall <u>fear every man his mother, and his father</u>, *and keep my sabbaths: I am the LORD your God.*

Leviticus 19:3 says that we are to fear our fathers and mothers. That means that we are to so respect them and what they expect from us, that we do not want to cause them grief or pain unnecessarily. We want to be obedient to them and bring them godly pleasure.

The prodigal son honoured passion before His parent (Father). In *Luke 15:11-32*. Let's just take a brief look at these verses.

Luke 15:13" *And not many days after the younger son gathered all together, and took his journey into a far country, and there wasted his substance with riotous living.*

[17] *And when he came to himself, he said, How many hired servants of my father's have bread enough and to spare, and I perish with hunger!*

[18] *I will arise and go to my father, and will say unto him, Father, I have sinned against heaven, and before thee,*

[19] *And am no more worthy to be called thy son: make me as one of thy hired servants.*

[20] *And he arose, and came to his father. But when he was yet a great way off, his father saw him, and had compassion, and ran, and fell on his neck, and kissed him.*

[21] *And the son said unto him, Father, I have sinned against heaven, and in thy sight, and am no more worthy to be called thy son.*

[22] *But the father said to his servants, Bring forth the best robe, and put it on him; and put a ring on his hand, and shoes on his feet:*

[23] *And bring hither the fatted calf, and kill it; and let us eat, and be merry:*

[24] *For this my son was dead, and is alive again; he was lost, and is found. And they began to be merry.*

[32] *It was meet that we should make merry, and be glad: for this thy brother was dead, and is alive again; and was lost, and is found."*

Passion will cause us to be as though we are dead before God; but respect will get His attention every time. The young man's passion led him into sin.

His passion brought him pain. His dishonouring of his father led him into a life of waste, and near destruction of himself. Some of us are like the prodigal son; its not until we are near destruction that we go to 'The Father'.

It's not till we can no longer cope with the wretched religious traditions that we have received that we long for that something more and reach out to find truth.

Truth that was under our noses all of the time. God wants us to come when things begin to go wrong, not when things get wrecked.

In the final words of the Old Testament **Malachi chapter 4**, here again God shows the direct repercussions of the practice of dishonouring your parents.

Malachi 4:4 "*Remember ye the law of Moses my servant, which I commanded unto him in Horeb for all Israel, with the statutes and judgments.*
[5] Behold, I will send you Elijah the prophet before the coming of the great and dreadful day of the LORD:
[6] And he shall turn the heart of the fathers to the children, and the heart of the children to their fathers, lest I come and smite the earth with a curse."

You can see that the breaking of this law results in bringing shame on your family name and ultimate destruction upon the lawbreaker.

Lack of respect for your parents dishonours your family and brings shame to its name and a curse upon the earth. The lack of respect for our earthly parents is a reflection of a far bigger problem of disrespect for the heavenly Father God.

In Summary then:

> **Honour your parents and you'll have a long life, dishonour them and you will die young. Could this be the reason why so many young people are dying today? Could it be they are dying because they are disrespectful?**
>
> **It's very simple, you give honour to father and mother and in return you get long life. If you don't you won't.**

CHAPTER 6

The law of preservation explained as survival – Law number 6

Exodus 20:13 Thou shalt not kill.

Now it is said, that those first five commandments are the commandments pertaining toward God. The next five are pertaining to our fellow man. You shouldn't murder - '*thou shalt not kill.*' No, not even with your tongue.

We know that this command was not simply against killing. It had a much more specific intent. However if we didn't kill each other, we would all live longer and hopefully have more fulfilling lives.

The meaning of it is to do with murder or deliberate killing, including the killing of a person's character with your tongue. Later in scripture, we find God giving Israel laws as to how to handle accidental killings.

So this law was not against killing in general. God simply wanted people to know that murder is out of bounds. Even character assassination.

The purpose of this law was not to forbid the killing of animals for food or other legitimate reasons. In the Old Testament God commanded animals for food and for sacrifices.

Christ ate meat at the Passover and fish as a part of a meal with the disciples. Through the scope and content of the scripture, we know that God is not saying that He is against the taking of life, yet He is clearly against murder.

For instance, the command does not forbid killing someone in self-defence.

***Exodus* 22:2** *"If a thief be found breaking up, and be smitten that he die, there shall no blood be shed for him"*.

God does not forbid capital punishment. In fact it was God who set this sanction in place before the scattering of the human race and before the law ***Genesis 9:6.***

Three note-worthy points about capital punishment is that it was God's command not man's, the commandment to kill all murderers was given before the law, and again at the time of the law.

This is a confirmation or establishing of the will of God to put away innocent blood from before Him by executing justice in His sight.

We can therefore say that God has fully confirmed His point of view as to what should happen to murderers about whom there is **'sure evidence'** that they did commit that crime.

I'm not talking about circumstantial evidence, nor yet about the evidence of one person. I'm talking about 'without a doubt' stuff. I'm speaking of the kind of killings where the guilt of the accused is without a shadow of a doubt.

The Bible says, **Numbers 35:30** "*Whoso killeth any person, the murderer shall be put to death by the mouth of witnesses: but* **one witness shall not testify against any person to cause him to die.**
[31] Moreover ye shall take no satisfaction for the life of a murderer, which is guilty of death: but he shall be surely put to death.
[32] And ye shall take no satisfaction for him that is fled to the city of his refuge, that he should come again to dwell in the land, until the death of the priest.
[33] So ye shall not pollute the land wherein ye are: for blood it defileth the land: and the land cannot be cleansed of the blood that is shed therein, but by the blood of him that shed it."

What this commandment actually forbids is murder. The taking of human life with intent to kill, and with wrong motives in our heart; is my personal definition of murder.

Suicide is a form of murder too. It's self-murder – You have no doubt been told it is self-release from the trials and difficulties of life. However it is hard to see how God gets glory from trials for trials sake; trials happen for a reason, and God gets glory only by bringing you out or through your trials.

God gets glory when He delivers you or keeps (preserves) you in the midst of your trials. Others will wonder how you can manage to overcome such a testing of your faith, and your answer will be, "By the grace of God". Therefore I exhort you 'do not commit suicide' it will send your soul straight to hell.

Only the devil will tell us to take our life or the life of another. Don't listen to him. How do you know that the day you take your life or murder another person is not the day of your miracle?

What goes for suicide goes for abortion too. Abortion is murder and murder is wrong. Now I do understand that there are some very 'good' reasons given by many for the termination of foetal life. But reason will not prevail above the commandments of God.

However with God there can be no excuse for killing an unborn child. A child who did not ask to come into this sin filled world, but who is incapable of defending its own rights. God is the champion of those who are unable to fight for themselves.

The blood of many unborn babies is 'crying out to God today' because of the sin we call abortion. Consider this; abortion may not be the only answer to your problem.

If your problem is an unwanted baby, what you really need is a 'wanting couple'. If your problem is a medical one perhaps what you need is a miracle. You may need a miracle, but you don't need a murder.

No one has the right to take life but the one who gave it. I'm not talking about the individual who gave birth, but the one who created that life. Only God has the right to take life. Can you create life? Then you have no right to take it. Give God the glory live and let live.

This command is written in order to help us humans to see the sanctity of human life in God's eyes. God wants us to put a high value on human life, because He does. Human life is valuable whether it is an unborn baby or an elderly person. The life of mankind whether foetal or full-grown is sacred to God.

Psalms 139:13 *"For thou hast possessed my reins: thou hast covered me in my mother's womb.*

[14] I will praise thee; for I am fearfully and wonderfully made: marvellous are thy works; and that my soul knoweth right well.

[15]My substance was not hid from thee, when I was made in secret, and curiously wrought in the lowest parts of the earth.

[16] Thine eyes did see my substance, yet being unperfect; and in thy book all my members were written, which in continuance were fashioned, when as yet there was none of them."

We are humans not mere animals as some would have us to believe. Man has an eternal soul. That's what makes us different. It is within the context to this commandment that the theory of evolution has a lot to answer for.

Evolution makes people believe that they originate among the animals, the inevitable conclusion of which is that since we come from animal ancestry, if we should behave like animals we can simply blame it on our origins and excuse our sins away.

Well I'm here to tell you that we did not come from the animals, we came from God. We were not evolved, but we were created. We were not meant to behave like animals, but like God because we were made in His image.

The sin of murder begins in the heart. **Mark 7:21** *tells us, "For from within, out of the heart of men, proceed evil thoughts, adulteries, fornications, murders,"*

Cain murdered his brother because he got angry at his brother's attitude toward God. He was angry because his brother's attitude was more honourable than his own attitude toward God. Put simply he was jealous of his brother, so he killed him.

Murder refers to an outward act that begins with an inward attitude.

***Matthew** 5:21 says, "Ye have heard that it was said by them of old time, Thou shalt not kill; and whosoever shall kill shall be in danger of the judgment:*
[22] But I say unto you, That whosoever is angry with his brother without a cause shall be in danger of the judgment: and whosoever shall say to his brother, Raca, shall be in danger of the council: but whosoever shall say, Thou fool, shall be in danger of hell fire."

If your inward attitudes drive you to anger, then you're not too far from murder. In fact sin lieth at the door. The Bible extends this thought by identifying hatred in the heart, as the same as the sin of murder.

***John** 1 3:15 "Whosoever hateth his brother is a murderer: and ye know that no murderer hath eternal life abiding in him."*

This is because if you hate someone enough it's a small thing to kill them. Whether with the tongue, a knife or a gun, it's still murder and if you hate someone, you will eventually try to kill them; one way or another.

Jesus told us that unholy anger and name-calling puts us in danger of committing the sin of murder; as surely as if we had taken a gun or knife already.

When someone takes life, they take the life of the individual killed and their children's life plus the life of their children's children. You will kill generations to come by murdering just one person.

Family feuds that lasted generations have started just this way. One individual after being killed by a member of another family left some problem unresolved the so that it festered and if it's not dealt with, the problem continues from generation to generation.

This kind of problem also exists where character assassination has occurred and if its not dealt with and put to death, there will always be a funny atmosphere of separation between yourself and the person you murdered in private with your tongue.

Anger and hatred are destructive emotions. They boil over into racial tension, marriage disputes, trade union clashes, riots, hooliganism, border and boundary disputes, vendettas between police and criminals, rival gang clashes, party political disputes.

Only the blood of Jesus can cleanse this and every other sin. The same blood that reconciles man to God, will reconcile man to man. Forgiveness is the key to applying the blood of Jesus in such a situation. Do not commit murder.

John I 1:7 "*But if we walk in the light, as he is in the light, we have fellowship one with another, and the blood of Jesus Christ his Son cleanseth us from all sin.*

[8] If we say that we have no sin, we deceive ourselves, and the truth is not in us.

[9] If we confess our sins, he is faithful and just to forgive us our sins, and to cleanse us from all unrighteousness."

In Summary the final thought of this Chapter is this:

> **Use your tongue right - speak life and forgive. Live and let live is all in a word and that word is in your mouth but starts in your heart. Anger, wrath, murder, slander. They all begin in your heart before they erupt as violent action. You have the opportunity to stop them before they manifest themselves. Do not murder!**

CHAPTER 7

The law of faithfulness explained as the law of fidelity – Law number 7

Exodus 20:14 Thou shalt not commit adultery.

You shouldn't commit adultery, not even with your eyes. If you never say yes with your eyes, then it will never be registered as yes with your heart.

If you never say yes with your eyes and your heart, then you'll never end up in bed committing adultery. For the eyes are the windows of the soul. Therefore we should set no wicked thing before our eyes and keep no wicked adulterous scene before your eyes.

When the eyes begin to stray its time to redirect our focus, because this is a sign which means that adultery is close at hand. Adultery is a sin of the sight.

It is the eyes that introduce us to this kind of sin, by triggering off strong latent desires. It is the looking that causes a problem in our heart.

Matthew 5:27 "Ye have heard that it was said by them of old time,

Thou shalt not commit adultery:

[28] But I say unto you, That __whosoever looketh__ on a woman to lust after her hath __committed adultery with her already in his heart__".

Marriage is the most sacred relationship that can exist between two human beings. God created one man for one woman for one lifetime. A Man and his wife were to enjoy each other's company for a whole lifetime. Each was to be committed to the other for life.

Marriage is a life thing. It's for life! If you're not willing to make this kind of commitment, then don't get married until you're ready and in the main time do not commit adultery. Incidentally if you're never ready to make that commitment, then just stay single and live right.

Sexual intercourse is one of the benefits and privileges of marriage. It is both a means of reproducing children and a source of pleasure. Some people want the benefits and privileges of marriage without the commitments and responsibilities.

That is just not possible. With God you can either have it all or not at all. God doesn't want us to play house, He wants us to build up and establish homes and godly families.

God created sex to take place only within the context of marriage and then only between Adams and Eves. That last statement outlaws homosexuality. God created Adam for Eve, not Eve for Evette and not Adam for Steve.

Any other form of sexual relationship except within one man and one life long mate of the opposite sex, joined together in matrimony is declared by the Bible as S.I.N.

Now you and I may not agree with this and we are entitled to our personal points of view, but my job in this book is to present God's point of view.

Through sex, husband and wife express the fullness of their love to each other and physically bond. To protect the sacredness of this, God gave the command, "thou shalt not commit adultery."

Strictly speaking, adultery is sexual intercourse between a married person and someone other than his/her married partner.

The Bible warns us against adultery and clearly calls this a sin. The thing about God is that He is not prejudices, racist or sexist. He says what He means and means what He says because he is the Creator.

Proverbs 6:27 *"Can a man take fire in his bosom, and his clothes not be burned?*

[28] Can one go upon hot coals, and his feet not be burned?

[29] So he that goeth in to his neighbour's wife; whosoever toucheth her shall not be innocent.

[30] Men do not despise a thief, if he steal to satisfy his soul when he is hungry;

[31] But if he be found, he shall restore sevenfold; he shall give all the substance of his house.

[32] But whoso committeth adultery with a woman lacketh understanding: he that doeth it destroyeth his own soul".

Sexual intercourse between a man and a woman, who are not married to anyone, is forbidden in scripture; and it is called fornication, but it still falls under the heading of adultery or sex sins.

That is what the adultery commandment is; it is the big umbrella for sex sins. However we must note that God is against all sex sins and has no special categories for a specific sex sin.

God is not more against one form of sex sin than another. He is against all forms of sex sins and against all forms of sin. Why? Because God is a Holy God, and cannot tolerate the presence, power and even the pull or attraction of sin.

Fornication is condemned in God's word, 1 *Corinthians 6:18,*

"Flee fornication. Every sin that a man doeth is without the body; but he that committeth fornication sinneth against his own body."

As with all other forms of sex sins including homosexuality (sex between two people of the same sex), bestiality (sex between a human and an animal).

Incest (sex between two people of the opposite sex who are closely related in blood lineage), Paedophilia (sex between an adult and a child), Masturbation (physical stimulation of the sex organs with the express purpose of achieving an orgasm).

Pornography is the possession of and attention to obscene photographs, stories, and other media for sexual gratification and pleasure.

Nudity in its literal form means to be without clothing, and many today do not consider this to be a problem. Enough to say that clothing was God's idea and not man's.

Whether you enjoy being nude or semi-nude, it would seem to indicate that either you take pleasure in the public display of your body; or you enjoy others taking pleasure in the public display of your body. God has a problem with this kind of attitude.

Nudity in God's eyes can be as simple as dressing in a way incompatible to God's requirements (God's Word) e.g. Adam and Eve after having sinned were dressed and yet God considered them naked and set about dressing them appropriately.

Though they were dressed in God's sight they were naked, because they were not covered in accordance with His word. God has standards of dress in the Old and New Testament. He has standards of dress applicable to the church and anyone dressed inadequately is to be considered naked in God's eyes.

Corinthians I 6:19 *"What? know ye not that your body is the temple of the Holy Ghost which is in you, which ye have of God, and ye are not your own?*

[20] For ye are bought with a price: therefore glorify God in your body, and in your spirit, which are God's"

Today, sexual impurity and perversion is tolerated by society at large and winked at, even smiled at, excused and taken lightly. However God's attitude has not changed He still hates sex sins.

1 Corinthians 6:9, *"Know ye not that the unrighteous shall not inherit the kingdom of God? Be not deceived:* **<u>neither fornicators</u>**, *nor idolaters, nor* **<u>adulterers</u>**, *nor* **<u>effeminate</u>**, *nor* **<u>abusers of themselves with mankind,</u>**

[10] Nor thieves, nor covetous, nor drunkards, nor revilers, nor extortioners, shall inherit the kingdom of God."

Is it not interesting to see that the first group of sins are mostly sex sins? Sex sins are high on God's priority list of sins that will keep you out of Heaven. Whenever we master sex sins, we do something that pleases God.

Strangely enough, you don't have to commit the act to be guilty of the sin of breaking this commandment. God judges not just our outward actions but also our thoughts and intents, **Matthew 5:27-28**. Jesus made a statement about a man who looks at a woman to lust after her, and declared that in the man's heart, he had already committed adultery.

Having said that, the outward appearance has a lot to do with sex sins. That's where the term 'dressed to kill' comes from. Lewd dressing incites or stimulates sex sins. While modest dressing is less likely to encourage or stimulate lustful behaviour and sex sins.

David is our best biblical example of the devastation caused by the sin of adultery, in:

*2 **Samuel 11:2** "And it came to pass in an eveningtide, that David arose from off his bed, and walked upon the roof of the king's house: and from the roof **he <u>saw a woman washing herself</u>**; and the woman was very beautiful to look upon.*
*[4] And David sent messengers, and **<u>took her; and she came in unto him, and he lay with her</u>**; for she was purified from her uncleanness: and she returned unto her house.*

[27] And when the mourning was past, David sent and fetched her to his house, and she became his wife, and bare him a son. **But the thing that David had done displeased the LORD."**

Observe what the sight of a naked body did to this man of God in his heart and it displeased God that he commit adultery and murder. Because of his carelessness, it caused him to lust, then to commit adultery and murder!

In the doing of this deed the man who is acknowledged as *"after God's heart"* displeased God intensely in his handling of this specific matter of adultery.

The Bible also speaks of the woman caught in adultery in:

Leviticus 20:10 *"And the man that committeth adultery with another man's wife, even he that committeth adultery with his neighbour's wife, the adulterer and the adulteress shall surely be put to death."*

There is a lesson to be learned from the experiences of those caught up in the sin of adultery. Sex sins cause devastation in the life of the persons who commit the sin and cause a breach of trust in the lives of connected partners.

God even introduced what could only be called the Jealousy law as a means of restoring confidence between a man and woman in a situation where there is suspicion of a breech of trust. He gave us a way under the Old Testament to maintain our confidence in the fidelity of the relationship and to be rewarded if we were wrongly accused.

It is important to note that every man in Old Testament times had the right to be jealous and to examine in a lawful way the faithfulness of his spouse.

Numbers 5:18 "*And the priest shall set the woman before the LORD, and uncover the woman's head, and put the offering of memorial in her hands, which is the jealousy offering: and the priest shall have in his hand the bitter water that causeth the curse:*

Numbers 5:19 *And the priest shall charge her by an oath, and say unto the woman, If no man have lain with thee, and if thou hast not gone aside to uncleanness with another instead of thy husband, be thou free from this bitter water that causeth the curse:*

Numbers 5:20 *But if thou hast gone aside to another instead of thy husband, and if thou be defiled, and some man have lain with thee beside thine husband:*

Numbers 5:27 *And when he hath made her to drink the water, then it shall come to pass, that, if she be defiled, and have done trespass against her husband, that the water that causeth the curse shall enter into her, and become bitter, and her belly shall swell, and her thigh shall rot: and the woman shall be a curse among her people.*

Numbers 5:28 *And if the woman be not defiled, but be clean; then she shall be free, and shall conceive seed.*

Numbers 5:29 *This is the law of jealousies, when a wife goeth aside to another instead of her husband, and is defiled;*"

Both extra-marital sex (sex outside of marriage) and pre-marital sex (sex before marriage) needs to be repented of. You need to make a decision that you will maintain your sexual purity if you are single. If it's worth having it's worth waiting for. Sex is beautiful in the right context.

Any man or woman who says that they love you and then encourages you to commit sex sins does not love you at all. Not even a little bit. What they really mean is they lust you. Lust is the desire to satisfy self at the expense of others.

Love on the other hand is the desire to meet the need of others even at the expense of self. Remember the principle of fidelity, that is, the privileges of marriage belong within the confines of marriage.

Not everyone will get married, but those who do need to uphold the sacredness of the contract of marriage. Those who do not need to get married need to understand and accept that the decision not to be married means they automatically forfeit the benefits of marriage for the benefits of singleness.

People living a single life while married or enjoying the benefits of a married life while single are the biggest hindrance today to godly personal relationships. We need to live the single life to its fullest while we are single and the married life when we are married.

None of us should look at marriage as something you try out. Many people display a thought pattern that says, "If it doesn't work we'll exchange it for a better one". In most if not all cases, better really means different.

That old saying "the grass always looks greener on the other side of the fence" seems to fit very neatly here. What most people fail to see is that a new relationship merely brings with it a different set of challenges and problems.

If you get your thinking into context, you will soon realise that it will not necessarily be better, just different. So is it worth an entire eternity just to taste something that is not better, but just in a different package?

What most people actually need is not a different relationship, or a new one; what is at the heart of such a desire is really for a better relationship. To get a better relationship, it takes work, it takes mutual commitment in order to improve the relationship we already have. It takes Christ!

The word that best summarises what makes personal relationships work is 'commitment'. Marriage is a part of the commitment process in a very special kind of personal relationship.

If our relationships are to be successful they must major in trusting each other. Trust can only be built on investments of faithfulness. When we are committed to each other, we are faithful to each other.

Because we are faithful to each other, we trust each other. Because we trust each other, we are committed to each other and on and on the circle of commitment goes on building until what we experience is a mature relationship that is high in trust and full of love.

> A faithful man shall abound with blessings, and faithfulness is what it takes to feel safe and secure in any relationship. Both parties need to be faithful and when this happens, the entire marriage abounds with the blessings of God.

CHAPTER 8

The laws of honesty explained as truth telling - Law number 8

Exodus 20:15 Thou shalt not steal.

You should not steal, this is not just physical, and it's also spiritual. Don't steal time from God by not praying, by not reading your Bible etc, don't steal God's money by not tithing, don't steal your family's time, don't steal by being deceptive or by cheating and cutting corners spiritual and natural.

Don't steal by being miserly and tight-fisted with your blessings that the Lord has given to you, or by using your work time for yourself. Do not steal at all.

Stealing is taking something that does not belong to you. Here are some facts concerning stealing. Stealing is stealing regardless of the amount or value of the thing you may be taking.

Stealing is stealing even though no one finds out. Stealing is a sin whether you steal from the rich or the poor. Stealing is wrong and therefore it is a sin.

Cheating in examinations, tests or otherwise is stealing, it's called stealing information. Receiving more than is due to you or saying nothing when you know you do not deserve something is also stealing.

To find money and not report it, but just to keep quiet is the sin of stealing. A person who does not pay their rightful debts is stealing. A person who cheats on income tax is stealing.

The scripture teaches that no thief shall enter into the kingdom of God. If you take anything and it doesn't belong to you no matter how small you won't enter the kingdom of God *1 Corinthians 6:10.* That is unless you restore what you stole. We must at least make an effort to set right whatever we have done wrong.

Both the Old and New Testament describe both sins of commission (Sins we commit by the wrong we do) and sins of omission (sins we commit by the good we did not do) as SIN.

Whether we failed to meet a need with our resources, or we stole something from someone less fortunate than ourselves, we are just as guilty.

Proverbs 3:27 "*Withhold not good from them to whom it is due, when it is in the power of thine hand to do it.*
[28] Say not unto thy neighbour, Go, and come again, and to morrow I will give; when thou hast it by thee."

James 4:17 "*Therefore to him that knoweth to do good, and doeth it not, to him it is sin.*"

We can steal from the less fortunate simply through inactivity when we could have helped and in the times we expressed miserliness when we could have been generous. This kind of inactivity is a crime in God's sight.

Lack of generosity in the sense of not giving your tithe or a proper sacrificial offering is also robbing God?

Malachi 3:8 *"Will a man rob God? Yet ye have robbed me. But ye say, Wherein have we robbed thee? In tithes and offerings.*

[9] Ye are cursed with a curse: for ye have robbed me, even this whole nation".

Do you remember Ahab's wrinkled brow when he made up his mind to steal Naboth's vineyard? How troubled he was? Thieves are often under great stress when they decide to take something.

Their conscience is shouting, this causes stress on the inside of such a person. Don't be stressed be blessed, stop stealing and start giving. The Bible teaches us to work with our hands and give. This is the answer to stealing.

The guilt of the sin of stealing can be forgiven if you repent and do what you can to make things right. In the Old Testament when a man stole something he was required to restore all plus 20% extra.

He also had to offer a trespass offering. He had to make things right with those wronged before his prayer was acceptable. This kind of surrendered attitude brought forgiveness. Surrender still saves us today. This is expressed in its fullness when we repent and seek to right our wrong.

No amount of weeping and saying sorry will do. Unless you are willing to make things right with those that have been wronged by you, you are not really ready to change.

You can now see that making things right brings them out in the open, it destroys your pride, takes things out of the realms of the darkness, and into the light. It makes you less likely to re-offend or even to wand to re-offend. Restoration is a definite deterrent to the sin of stealing.

Who in their right mind will want to go through making all things public and not mean business? To re-offend would only cause greater embarrassment than the original sin. This being too painful for our ego, it makes us less likely to want to offend or re-offend.

With theft, God is not interested in the size of your sacrifice; He is only interested in a contrite and broken heart. A heart that is willing to do what ever it takes to make things right.

No amount of giving can right a theft only repentance, reconciliation and restoration. Thou shalt not steal, at least not if you want to go to heaven.

> **Honesty is the best policy**

Law number 9 – The law of authenticity explained as being genuine or real.

Exodus 20:16 Thou shalt not bear false witness against thy neighbour.

You should not bear false witness against thy neighbour. One obvious category of this sin is being false. Pretending you like your neighbour when in fact you loathe them. Do not slander by spreading gossip and false reports that destroys the reputation of another.

Say that, which is true and verifiable, speaks the truth in full and not in part. Do not remain silent or act ignorant of facts and thereby mislead. Only say you know when you do. Only say you saw when you did. Only say you have when you do.

Bearing false witness is a sin of ease. For it is 'taking the easy path that makes men and rivers crooked.' This sin also has a close connection to tale-bearing, gossiping, criticising and backbiting.

Two common violations of this command are - Lying and slander. Lying is saying or acting out that which is false or untrue.

Lying is misrepresenting the truth. It is bearing false witness of the truth before God. It is commonly called 'telling fibs or little white lies'. Lying also includes making exaggerated claims or embellishing stories by adding to or extending the details of an actual event.

Remaining quiet to falsely take credit is also a form of lying. A subtle change in tone, an inflection or expression designed to be misleading is as the boldest darkest lie. As a point of fact, let it be known that there are no 'little white lies.' A lie is a lie, and that's the measure of it.

It is far easier to lie than to tell the truth, especially when you are under pressure or you are forced to respond unprepared or quickly. It is easier to lie when the implications for telling the truth are fearful.

Therein dwells the attraction of this sin. It is the easy way out. However lying is wrong, no matter what shade of lie it is. It registers in heaven and hell as the same sin of ease – Lying.

Even totally otherwise spiritual people lie, e.g. Peter lied under pressure about knowing Jesus,

Mark 14:67 "And when she saw Peter warming himself, she looked upon him, and said, And thou also wast with Jesus of Nazareth.
[68] But he denied, saying, I know not, neither understand I what thou sayest. And he went out into the porch; and the cock crew.
[69] And a maid saw him again, and began to say to them that stood by, This is one of them.
[70] And he denied it again. And a little after, they that stood by said again to Peter, Surely thou art one of them: for thou art a Galilaean, and thy speech agreeth thereto.
[71] But he began to curse and to swear, saying, I know not this man of whom ye speak."

It is unfortunate, but God considers everyone who practices lying as siding with Satan who is called *'the father of lies'*. This is an area where we must be very diligent.

If we have a lying habit, we must overcome it with a truth-telling habit. For the scriptures cannot be broken, *"all liars shall have their part in the lake of fire."* Revelations 21:8.

The second aspect of bearing false witness is slander. Slander is spreading gossip and false reports that destroy the reputation of another. Spreading gossip has three very deadly effects.

Firstly it poisons the mind of the one who gossips. Secondly it poisons the mind of the one who hears the gossip and finally it damages the reputation of the one who is gossiped about.

"Speak no evil hear no evil" Seems like a good policy when this sin rears its head. The reason God hates false witness so much is because it was lying that brought sin into the world. This makes it an important part of a package of sins that God distinctly hates.

Proverbs 6:19 "*A false witness that speaketh lies, and he that soweth discord among brethren*".

There are 3 kinds of lies that we can tell. We may lie by saying something that is not true. We may lie by telling the truth but only voicing part of the matter.

Thirdly we can lie simply by remaining silent and act as though ignorant concerning the facts with <u>intent to mislead</u> others, especially when we are questioned on the matter, this constitutes lying.

It is not that there is anything wrong with silence, it's the staying quiet and holding back facts in order to mislead others and pass off responsibility which rightly belongs to us.

God is a God of truth, whether white lies, social lies, the business lie or lies of convenience a lie is a lie, and God hates lies.

Revelations 21:27, *"Neither whatsoever works abomination or makes a lie."* David said, *"I have chosen the way of truth"*.

Truth telling is a choice. Make it your choice and God will give you the grace to do it. Truth will uphold you and defend you against your enemies in the darkness of a world filled with deception. Remember God can only defend truth.

When we lie we tie God's hands and loose the devil to speak in our situation we should fight the devil by truth telling and loose God, into our lives we need to tell the truth as a matter of lifestyle.

The only way to overcome the habit of lying is to replace it with a habit of truth telling all liars must change their lifestyle.

> **Be real - tell the truth.**

CHAPTER 9

The law of satisfaction explained as fulfilment - Law number 10

Exodus 20:17 *Thou shalt not covet thy neighbour's house, thou shalt not covet thy neighbour's wife, nor his manservant, nor his maidservant, nor his ox, nor his ass, nor any thing that is thy neighbour's.*

You shouldn't covet your neighbour's goods. To covet means to have a strong desire or liking for something that belongs to someone else. It is a sin of passion, it requires the investment of our emotions; in particular the sin of covetousness is like idolatry it seeks to engage our love.

It hunts for our heart's affections. When these are found so is the way of our destruction paved. Satan knows by experience that if he gets our heart he's got the whole of us.

So he searches for our weaknesses by seeking to know what exactly we would covet. Then he springs the trap. All this happens because of covetousness.

This is the sin of greed in action. It is a direct challenge, to the love we ought to have for God. It is the sin at the heart of gambling (By the way **the lottery is gambling**). If we do not covet we will not be greedy or materialistic, we will not desire what we either have no rights to, or did not work for.

Coveting is an inward sin, a sin of the thought life and of the emotions. You can do it and no one but you and God will ever know.

Sometimes even you will not recognise that you're being covetous. This sin is so subtle. God hates it; it is a secret sin. You can covet a person's good looks, money or possessions, someone's wife, husband or even someone's position and they need never find out.

Covetousness is the root of all sin i.e *"**the love** of money is the root of all evil"*. E.g. Adam and Eve were overcome by covetousness when they ate of the forbidden fruit.

The serpent told Eve she should desire the fruit and what it could do for her. Adam desired Eve above even God. Through the subtle suggestion of the devil, covetousness took away Adam and Eve's relationship with God.

More than anything the devil uses advertising to stir up covetousness in people today. Often times if you never saw something advertised either you would not think that you needed it or you would not have brought that brand.

The advert stirred up your latent desires and you felt that you just had to have it. Often the devil uses advertising another way; he uses it to keep covetousness alive.

Many a person would have forgotten about their desire for cigarettes, alcohol or some other sinful habit, after having made a decision to give it up.

They were perfectly contented until having seen an advert involving their weakness they proceeded to sin either immediately or a short time afterwards. Please do not underestimate the power of wrongly directed desire.

Covetousness always leads to other sins. Looking back at Adam, his covetousness caused him to disobey and rebel against God; it caused him to lie. For David covetousness caused him to steal, commit adultery, lie and commit murder.

Covetousness is a major gateway to greater sin; if you do not have the "want-to", it is absolutely impossible for the devil to cause you to sin except it be accidentally or out of ignorance. However wrongly directed desire is dangerous to us all. Desire put together with wrongly framed opportunities will give birth to sin.

David probably had a desire for sexual gratification on the night that he looked out of the window and saw Bathsheba. As a result of a desire and a wrongly framed opportunity, sin came to his home that night to the uttermost. It ruined the reputation of an otherwise godly man and a godly lifestyle.

Covetousness is what caused the Jews of Nehemiah's day to sin against God. It caused them to break the Sabbath to make money – though they would have said they were simply trying to make a living. Can you now see how covetousness seeks to clothe itself in the shroud of practicality, **Nehemiah 13:15-21**

Sometimes it even dresses itself up in the cloths of righteousness. For instance just look at the lottery, don't they appear to be seeking this same shrouding (respectability and acceptance) by giving vast sums to charity while encouraging a whole nation to sin by gambling.

This rationale is plain old unacceptable to God; the problem is labelled Covetousness; its out working is greed and the end result is death. *"For the wages of sin is death "* **Romans 6:23**.

In the Bible a covetous person is called an "idolater" because he makes money his God.

Luke 12:15 *"And he said unto them, Take heed, and beware of covetousness: for a man's life consisteth not in the abundance of the things which he possesseth."*

The Bible lists covetousness with the worst sins possible that we may know the seriousness of the crime. ***1 Corinthians 6:9-10.***

Covetousness leads to other sins. It opens the floodgate to sin and multiplies itself against itself. Covetousness destroys family ties, and entire families. Achan could not have supposed how things would turn out for him and his family when he made up his mind to covet and steal the Babylonish garment and gold from the booty in Jericho, ***Joshua Chapter 7***.

The greatest safe guard you can develop against covetousness is to lose your strong hold on your wallet, be more generous and Love God with all of your heart. Practice being more generous.

Always remember that a tight fist will cut off your blood supply. Through covetousness whole churches are blinded to the existence of the lost and fail to please God because they don't know how to give of their time, treasury or talents in the service of the Lord.

The devil literally offered Jesus the whole world as his inheritance. If Jesus had just become a Satan worshiper, the devil would have given Him the world as a reward.

That offer was an appeal to any possible covetousness in Jesus' life. But Jesus pointed out that His love and adoration was only for God. Thank God Jesus resisted becoming covetous, and as a result we have this great salvation.

The tenth commandment leaves the 'forever desiring' Adamic race 'weighed in the balance and found wanting'. Instead of always grasping for more, Paul encouraged us to be satisfied with what we have, *"Godliness with contentment is great gain." 1Timothy 6:6-8.*

> **Be satisfied with what you got, let your eyes see and not long for what it beholds. What we see should go to our eyes and not to our hearts.**

The Summary of the 10 Commandments
So the 10 Commandments are the only part of the Law, spoken by God's audible voice to Israel. As to whether Go would have said more audibly, who knows?

It would have seem to have been God's intention. A further 45 commandments are yet given on the mount, right up until *Exodus 23:33*, WHERE Moses descends from the mountain.

In *Exodus 24:3*, Moses tells all the words of the Lord to the people, and in verse 4, he writes down the words of the Lord.

"Exodus 24:4 And Moses wrote all the words of the LORD, and rose up early in the morning, and builded an altar under the hill, and twelve pillars, according to the twelve tribes of Israel."

By now some of you probably feel thoroughly condemned. It is certainly not the intent of this book to condemn anyone, but it is the end result of the working of the Law. This is what the Law was designed to do by God.

It is supposed to expose sin, it is designed to make a man to know that he is a sinner and in need of help. We cannot in our flesh fulfil the law, it is an absolute impossibility. The purpose of the law is to condemn us of sin by showing us our lack of righteousness.

The Law shows us our weaknesses, and in the light of this everyone knows that they need something more. That something more is Jesus Christ. Stay with me a little longer on this line of exploration.

There are some more things we must open up in this area before we can come into the richness of the true rest that God has given to us.

However I can promise you that as the Law works to reveal our need, later on in this book the power of Christ through the Spirit of God will reveal our strength in Him.

The breaking of the law always led to death. The main point about the law is that it is designed by God to be death to the sinner.

This is the reason for its existence to be judge and executioner of sin and sinners. We must never lose sight of this fact. The law of the Old Testament comprises largely of two parts:

1. The Old Testament rituals in the tabernacle including its sacrifices of 'bulls and goats' and its attendance by the Aaronic priesthood who served at its altars.

2. The Ten Commandments with its statutory requirements of ordinances and do's and don'ts. The Law says, Thou shalt not, and thou shalt.

Most Christians do not have a problem accepting that we are not under the first aspect of the law. Forever Jesus is the Lamb of God that takes away the sins of the world. This was a once in a lifetime transaction. His sacrifice put an end to the need for animal sacrifice once and for all.

It is the validity of the other laws, sometimes called moral laws and in particular the requirement to keep the Sabbath that many find controversial.

The entire Old Covenant; was destined to be replaced by another contract that had improved conditions. It would be a covenant that would never become old. Unlike the first it would be eternal. It would be based upon better precepts and it would have a lasting purpose.

The simple message of the law is that not one person can ever be made righteous by keeping it, Galatians 2:16-17. In comparing that last statement with scripture it does not take long before we realise that after 40 years of wondering a whole nation died out while performing the rituals of the law and adhering to the letter.

Only two men of that generation entered into God's promise. They entered in because they were different from the rest.

These two men Joshua and Caleb were heroes of faith. We therefore conclude that what could not be achieved by the law, was achieved by faith.

In summary: The answer to the law is very simple

> 'Have Faith in God'. Faith in God is not faith in your abilities or your possessions, your goodness or your personality or qualifications. Faith in God is dependent upon what He can do through you that you could not do for or through self. Therefore know that you can rely upon Him and depend on Him because He will never let you down.

CHAPTER 10

The foundation of the law - the Old Testament

Now God was speaking to all Israel, and after Ten Commandments, the people of Israel begged Him to stop. The people of Israel were petrified; they were scared stiff lest they should die from having encountered God.

They all saw the mountain on fire and the smoke coming out from the fire. They could all hear the thunderous voice, but they could see no form.

They couldn't see God they only heard his voice. It's times like this when typically the people of God appreciate a mediator or go between man and God.

For the first time they started running to Moses. Instead of criticising and complaining about Moses, they asked Moses to talk to God on their behalf, because they were afraid. They begged God to stop speaking, so He stopped.

The people's hearts had begun to melt, they were afraid for their lives and so God stopped at commandment number ten. Moses said, "This is why God appeared to you so that He might prove you (test you).

To know whether you would fear him". The people asked Moses to speak as their representative, they asked him to speak to God, and let God speak to him.

He was then to come and teach them what God had said. In the strength of this agreement Moses went away and God related to him some 613 precepts of the law.

Moses went up the mountain Exodus chapter 20, and after communing with God he came down in **Exodus Chapter 24**.

Exodus 24:3 "And Moses came and told the people all the words of the LORD, and all the judgments: and all the people answered with one voice, and said, **All the words which the LORD hath said will we do.**

[4] And Moses wrote all the words of the LORD, and rose up early the morning, and builded an altar under the hill, and twelve pillars, according to the twelve tribes of Israel.

[5] And he sent young men of the children of Israel, which offered burnt offerings, and sacrificed peace offerings of oxen unto the LORD.

[6] And Moses took half of the blood, and put it in basins; and half of the blood he sprinkled on the altar.

[7] And he took **the book of the covenant**, *and read in the audience of the people: and they said, All that the LORD hath said will we do, and be obedient.*

[8] And Moses **took the blood, and sprinkled it on the people**, *and said,* **Behold the blood of the covenant, which the LORD hath made with you** *concerning all these words". (Compare these words with those of Christ:* **Matthew 26:28**).

So Moses came down, and in **verse 3**, Moses told all the people the words God gave him to relay to them and in **verse 4**, Moses then wrote it down and then dedicated the covenant.

When we see the covenant and the way it was given, it was of primary importance that it be dedicated by blood. We also realise that this was an agreement that Israel needed to remember, so God gave them something to remember it with - the Sabbath day and blood.

These two instruments of remembrance were given by God to the nation of Israel in order to impact their consciousness. One memorial was the immediate sight and smell of so much blood.

Imagine having that sprinkled on you, the stains on your clothing, the ambience; oh what an imprint that would all make on your memory. God got their attention and they were to remember that day they cut covenant with God.

The second instrument of remembrance was subtler; it was to be an abiding witness of the covenant they cut that day. Something that they were supposed to do regularly that would remind them of that covenant.

God chose the Sabbath day as such a reminder. Every time they kept that day they were to think back to the covenant and make that day a time of covenant renewal.

So in **Exodus 24 verse 8**, we see that *"The covenant"*, was sealed with blood. Now remember that statement; *"Behold the Blood of the Covenant."* As we go on, God was not finished with Moses yet therefore in **verse 12**, God spoke to Moses?

Exodus 24:12 "And the LORD said unto Moses, Come up to me into the mount, and be there: and I will give thee tables of stone, and a law, and commandments which I have written; that thou mayest teach them."

This is the first time the Commandments are to be written down.

So Moses went up and God began to show him the Ark of the Covenant, the Mercy Seat and all the different dimensions that He had designed and everything that He wanted Moses to ensure was made.

There is a parallel here that throughout God's instructions and dealings with mankind, we see that God is always very specific. He leaves nothing to chance and makes Himself clear in accordance with man's needs.

Beware of people who say, "It doesn't matter how you do things in life as long as you are happy? After all if we make mistakes, God understands!"

If you read **Exodus chapter 24** when Moses went up in the mountain and you read Exodus 25 about how God really goes into the specific details of what He expects Moses to get done. You will soon understand that God is a God of detail and expects man to do what He has asked of him in exactly the way He requested that it be done.

Exodus 25:9 "*According <u>to all that I show thee, after the pattern</u> of the tabernacle, and the pattern of all the instruments thereof, <u>even so shall ye make it</u>*.

Exodus 25:40 And look that thou <u>make them after their pattern, which was showed thee in the mount.</u>

God is a God of clarity. God told Moses how He wanted the mercy seat made, how He wanted the Ark of Covenant constructed and He went on in great detail to say exactly what He did and did not want.

God was very specific. God told Moses to make sure that he did everything "according to the pattern" that He had shown him.

God left a special pattern he said, "You make sure you do everything according to the pattern, which I have left you." God is still telling Mankind to follow the pattern of His word.

In every area of concern that man can have, God has already left us a pattern, all that is required is that man should seek. If you seek, you shall find in His Word the promises that make the pattern clear.

Moses up the mountain and down again
Moses was up in the mountain in attentive communion with God. And God continued relaying the different commandments He had for Israel to Moses; who would in time bring them down the Mountain and teach them to Israel.

Exodus 31:12 "And the LORD spake unto Moses, saying,

[13] Speak thou also unto the children of Israel, saying, Verily my sabbaths ye shall keep: for it is a sign between me and you throughout your generations; that ye may know that I am the LORD that doth sanctify you".

The searching questions for sincere seekers are, for whom does the Word of God say the Sabbath is a sign? Who is God speaking to? God is speaking to Moses about telling His commandments to the Children of Israel.

So we know the Children of Israel are the subject of this Word from God. It is in this context that God says, *"My Sabbath is a sign between me and the children of Israel."* Am I twisting the Scripture or is that what it says? That's what it says.

Exodus 31:14 *"Ye shall keep the sabbath therefore; for it is holy unto you: every one that defileth it shall surely be put to death: for whosoever doeth any work therein, that soul shall be cut off from among his people."*

Cut off from among which people? Failure to obey the law, would lead to being disinherited and stoned from among the children of Israel of course. Failure to keep the law demands death, the death of the person responsible for breaking the Law.

Exodus 31:16 *"Wherefore the **children of Israel shall keep the sabbath, to observe the sabbath throughout their generations, for a perpetual covenant**.*
*[17] It is a **sign between me and the children of Israel forever**: for in six days the LORD made heaven and earth, and on the seventh day he rested, and was refreshed."*

Moses had been up the mountain with God, now he would come down the mountain to pain and heart break. The people he had left in charge would disappoint him and let God down.

The people he had led would now be found to have rebelled against God and be in sin. What would be the result of this when Moses sees it?

Exodus 32:15 And Moses turned, and went down from the mount, and the two tables of the testimony were in his hand: the tables were written on both their sides; on the one side and on the other were they written.

[16] And the tables were the work of God, and **the writing was the writing of God, graven upon the tables.**

What Moses brought down from the Mount Sinai were not ten suggestions, but Ten Commandments that demanded obedience or judgement.

If the people would not obey they then these Commandments would cease to be blessings and become curses to these same people. These commandments were not man's idea but God's.

Contained in the midst of these ten, would be the fourth commandment. But we must never forget that the fourth commandment is not the law, it is only a part of the law. Which Moses was to relay to God's people Israel.

It would be the whole Law that would be broken, and even those that broke only one point of the law would be judged by all of the Law. Why? because its the whole law that was important to God.

As Moses descends the mountain, we can only assume at this point that it is the Ten Commandments that he is bringing, because they are not called the Ten Commandments in the scriptures at this point.

We see the tablets (tablets of stone) Moses is bringing down the mountain are written on both sides. There are two tables of stone, and God wrote what was on them on both sides of the tablets. Moses approached the camp of Israel, with these two tables of stone in his hands.

While Moses was still up in the mountain communing with God about what he would deliver to the people on behalf of God. Israel had back-slidden and started to commit idolatry with the golden calf.

Since Moses had a way of loosing his temper quickly when he saw the state that the people were in spiritually, he lost every ounce of his cool and broke the tables of stone in a rage.

It is in this setting that Israel broke their Covenant with God, and committed idolaty. For their sin, God punished Israel and again Moses had to intercede for Israel to prevent God from wiping them out.

Israel responded by consecrating themselves and gathering at Mount Horeb, *Exodus 33:4-7*.

The Second time around
Once again God spoke to Moses in Chapter 34 verse 1, He said to Moses, "***Hew thee two tables of stone like unto the first:*** *and I will write upon these tables the words that were in the first tables, which thou brakest.*" After this Moses went up into Mount Sinai, and God renewed His covenant with Moses and Israel.

God makes a point of noting that it was Moses who broke the 'Covenantal tablets' for this is a type of what was to happen with the first Covenant. It is man who broke of failed to keep the first Covenant. *"After this manner (says God) I will make another covenant with you and Israel, and he wrote upon the tables of stone"*

Exodus 34 verse 28 said, *"and he wrote upon the tables the words of the covenant the Ten Commandments."*

Exodus 34 verse 28 is the first mention of the Ten Commandments it is the very first time it's ever been mentioned and the Bible calls it, ***"The Ten Commandments the words of the Covenant."***

Now later Moses comes down from this mountain with the Ten Commandments in his hands but he didn't realise that something about him had changed.

When he came down the people looked at him and they were astonished because his face shone. It shone so much that the people could not look on him without covering their eyes.

So Moses had to get a veil and put it over his face so that when he was talking to Israel so that he would not frighten them by his striking appearance.

He used a veil for covering the brightness of his face. Since he was constantly in the presence of the Lord, the glory of God was upon him and he had changed. This has a comparison in the New Testament.

The comparison is that while the Old Testament was not obeyed by man, and could not affect anyone's moral behaviour from the inside. The New Testament through the power of God's Spirit would accomplish through access to the hearts of men.

So Moses because of the change that had taken place in him had to cover his face with the veil when he was in the presence of the people.

He would remove it when he was in the presence of God, with no other person around. I'm saying all these things because they are very significant when you speak about the Ten Commandments.

The weakness of any covenant however is that it can be broken. A covenant is only a covenant when both parties enter into it by free will and choose to be bound by the conditions of the contract. In the same way they enter into it by choice, they can choose to break it also.

But in breaking it, they invoke all the curses and contrary conditions that were written into the contract. This is what would happen to Israel. Because of the breaking of the covenant God would choose to turn away and in fact that's what **Roman 11** says.

Romans 11:5 *Even so then at this present time also there is a remnant according to the election of grace.*
[6] And if by grace, then is it no more of works: otherwise grace is no more grace. But if it be of works, then is it no more grace: otherwise work is no more work.

[7] What then? Israel hath not obtained that which he seeketh for; but the election hath obtained it, and the rest were blinded

[8] (According as it is written, God hath given them the spirit of slumber, eyes that they should not see, and ears that they should not hear;) unto this day.

[9] And David saith, Let their table be made a snare, and a trap, and a stumblingblock, and a recompense unto them:

[10] Let their eyes be darkened that they may not see, and bow down their back alway.

[11] I say then, Have they stumbled that they should fall? God forbid: but rather through their fall salvation is come unto the Gentiles, for to provoke them to jealousy.

[12] Now if the fall of them be the riches of the world, and the diminishing of them the riches of the Gentiles; how much more their fulness?"

God it says, in the scripture in essence has now turned from Israel – Why? Because they failed to keep the Covenant made between themselves and God. It also tells us that God has not turned form them forever.

Instead it is just for a time that blindness has come upon them. This cutting off of Israel has allowed many today to be saved, so we know that their reconciling will bring an even greater glory to God.

Continuing with our look into *Exodus 34: 1-4*. Notice and compare that with the breaking of the first two tablets in Exodus 24. These two scriptures make a representation of the breaking of the first covenant by Israel. Observe if you will that it's not the first covenant that survives, but it is the second.

It is the Second Covenant, which is a type of the New Testament that survives. It will be the New Testament that survives along the ages. What we find in the scriptures above is when Moses came down from the mountain the second time, he was no longer the same.

Notice the change had not happened with the first two tables but through the second two. With the two tablets of stone that he was first given he remained normal but with the second two tablets his countenance changed. Everything about him changed.

The second two tablets, which Moses received upon Mount Sinai are a type of the New Testament that produces change in our hearts. Change that the Old Testament cannot give to us.

The new covenant that God has made with man will utterly change us, so that we are never the same again and others will realise it when they look at us, when they talk to us, when they live with us.

Now remember the Ten Commandments were called," *the very word of the Covenant*", and so moving on then through to Deuteronomy; Moses in his speech is going back to the time when God gave them the word of the Covenant which is known as the Ten Commandments.

In **Deuteronomy 4 verse 13** Moses is speaking and says , "*And he declared unto you his covenant, which he commanded you to perform, even **ten commandments** (second mention); and he wrote them upon two tables of stone*"

A memorial of Egypt
In **Deuteronomy chapter 5 verse 2** '**The Lord our God made a Covenant with us**; *The Lord made not this covenant with our fathers but with us even us who are all of us here alive this day.*'

What Moses was pointing out is that before the time of Mount Sinai the Ten Commandments was never given to anybody before the Children of Israel at Sinai. God made that covenant with them right there in the wilderness.

Deuteronomy 5:12 *"Keep the sabbath day to sanctify it, as the LORD thy God hath commanded thee"*

Deuteronomy 5:15" *And remember that thou wast a servant in the land of Egypt, and that the LORD thy God brought thee out thence through a mighty hand and by a stretched out arm**: therefore the LORD thy God commanded thee to keep the sabbath day**.*"

> **From this scripture reference we can safely say that the Sabbath was given by God to commemorate Israel's deliverance from Egypt.**

In the same way as God never made a covenant with the forefathers of Israel who died in Egypt. God did not make a covenant with the Gentiles at this time either. So they had no covenant rights before God.

The Old Covenant or Testament is a covenant between God and the Jews whom Moses brought out of Egypt and into the wilderness. In other words – The Gentiles have no part in the Old Testament or Covenant. This Old Covenant would be a memorial to God's deliverance of a nation out of Egypt.

The Ten Commandments was not given to anybody before Mount Sinai. And in Deuteronomy Chapter 5 verse 15 God explains why He did things this way.

He has a way of giving a deeper revelation a bit at a time here a little there a little, word upon word, and line upon line, precept upon precept. First he reminds them, "I brought you out of Egypt." Then He uses this as the justification why they should simply rest.

In other words God is saying to them, "the reason why I gave you the Sabbath is so that you will always remember what I did in Egypt and you will never forget that I the Lord your God delivered you from the hands of the Egyptians. I wonder if you see the point that I am making? Let's try to make it clear with an example.

Let us suppose for a moment that the Chinese communists, turned around tomorrow and said, 'from now on every Tibetan will have to celebrate D-Day'.

I think there would be a lot of Tibetans scratching their heads, because they would be wondering what D-Day was, and what it had to do with them? It means nothing to the Tibetans, nothing at all.

They were not involved in the war in Europe, so why should they celebrate the victory? What would be the point of asking them to celebrate D-Day?

Now for the European countries that overcame the perils of Hitler's Germany and those who remembered the sacrifices that they had to make in order to win the precious freedoms that we enjoy today, to them it would mean something to celebrate, it would mean remembering D-day.

For the Jews the Sabbath is like that, it means something to them. They were delivered from slavery in Egypt, so they have a reason to celebrate. They had nowhere to live and God gave them the promised-land for a home.

They were a people who were not a people and God became their God and their king. But to Gentiles what would be the purpose of keeping the Sabbath?

Now God says, in essence, "I gave you the Sabbath that you will remember that I your God delivered you from the hands of Egypt."

Now I ask you, what would be the point of the Gentiles celebrating the Passover? It means nothing to us. We don't know what Egypt looked like.

We weren't under the slavery of the Egyptians, it means nothing to us, so there was no way in God's mind that He was giving the Sabbath in part or full to anyone outside the children of Israel to celebrate, and that's the message.

This being so it seems logical to conclude that the Sabbath was never given for any Gentile to keep it was only given to the children of Israel. They were to keep it as a memorial of God's deliverance from their bondage in Egypt.

Now Moses spoke these words in **Deuteronomy 9:9**, "When I was gone up into the mount to receive <u>*the tables of stone, even the tables of the covenant which the LORD made with you*</u>, *then* I abode in the mount forty days and forty nights, I neither did eat bread nor drink water:"

(Notice that Moses keeps calling the tables of stone "*the tables of the covenant or the words of the covenant or the tables of the testimony*").

Deuteronomy 9:11 "And it came to pass at the end of forty days and forty nights, that **the LORD gave me the two tables of stone, even the tables of the covenant.**"

Deuteronomy 9:15" So I turned and came down from the mount, and the mount burned with fire: **and the two tables of the covenant were in my two hands**"

In **Deuteronomy 10 verse 4**, comes the third mention of the Ten Commandments.

"<u>**And he wrote on the tables**</u>, according to the first writing, <u>**the ten commandments**</u>, which the LORD spake unto you in the mount out of the midst of the fire in the day of the assembly: <u>**and the LORD gave them unto me.**</u>"

So the Ten Commandments are mentioned 3 times - ***Exodus 34:28; Deuteronomy 4:13; and 10:4***. Called the '*tables of the Covenant*'' They are called the covenant because they were the sum total of the entire contract between God and Israel at Sinai.

What I am trying to say is that there is no way scripturally you can separate the ten commandments from the rest of the law because out of the ten commandments came the other 600 plus, laws of the Jewish people.

Apparently there are some 613 laws and all these are derived from the Ten Commandments. So the Ten Commandments were the sole basis of all the 613 laws.

They could all have been summed up in the Ten Commandments. So when a Jew thinks of the Ten Commandments he thinks of the whole substance of the law, and not just the ten word or commands.

The Ten Commandments are the embodiment of the Law. They represent all of the law. Therefore are they called interchangeably the Law of Moses and the Law of God.

The Jews today in general do not recognise, the New Testament because they do not recognise Jesus as their Messiah. However we accept Jesus and we should also accept His Covenant with the World as the exclusive grounds of our walk with Him.

When A Jew hears of 'the covenant', he immediately thinks of the Old Covenant. At the mention of the word covenant, he thinks of Mount Sinai where God gave them the Ten Commandments.

From this we realise that the covenant the one God made with Israel in the wilderness is based on the Ten Commandments and it is His Covenant with the Jews.

Romans 10:5 "For Moses describeth <u>the righteousness which is of the law</u>, That the man <u>which **doeth those things**</u> shall live by them."

Deuteronomy 6:25 "And it shall be our righteousness, if we <u>**observe to do all these commandments**</u> before the LORD our God, as he hath commanded us."

Leviticus 18:4 "Ye shall **do <u>my judgments, and keep mine ordinances</u>**, to walk therein: I am the LORD your God.
[5] Ye shall therefore <u>**keep my statutes, and my judgments**</u>: which if a man do, he shall live in them: I am the LORD".

Jeremiah 7:23 "But this thing commanded I them, saying, <u>**Obey my voice**</u>, and I will be your God, and ye shall be my people: and <u>**walk ye in all the ways that I have commanded you**</u>, that it may be well unto you".

'Observing God's commandments', 'doing God's judgements and keeping His ordinances and statutes', are together called by the apostle Paul, *'the works of the law'*. The verses above say the same thing in essence, it's saying that we are to act in accordance with God's commandments and statutes.

If we obey them they will constitute our righteousness (Romans 10), our living (Deuteronomy 6), our living (Leviticus 18) and our well-being (Jeremiah 7).

Now these three things - righteousness, daily living and well-being together make up just about all that we are looking for in our Christian life.

Yet what it promised could only be received by faith. This is one of the anomalies of the Old Testament that even under the law, if a man lived by faith it would be accounted to him for righteousness.

Romans 4:1 *"What shall we say then that Abraham our father, as pertaining to the flesh, hath found?*

[2] For if Abraham were justified by works, he hath whereof to glory; but not before God.

[3] For what saith the scripture? Abraham believed God, and it was counted unto him for righteousness.

[4] Now to him that worketh is the reward not reckoned of grace, but of debt.

[5] But to him that worketh not, but believeth on him that justifieth the ungodly, his faith is counted for righteousness."

So in summary, the law says, "Obey the commandments and be faithful to all the ordinances and statutes and it will be your righteousness, your living and your well-being".

The Law is only found recorded in two of the books written by Moses - Exodus 20 and Deuteronomy 5. These are the only aspects of the Law that was written and engraved on the two tables of stone. We have also found that that it was written to Israel and not to the Gentiles

> **The foundation of the law is the 10 commandments the New Testament builds on this foundation through the introduction of grace and an explanation of faith, God takes the laws and writes them on our hearts. He gives us something to look forward to. Until then man had no hope, because his ability to deal with sin was limited to his own strength. However with the giving of the Holy Ghost, came the ability to overcome sin and to live a life pleasing to God through the laws written and engraved upon our hearts.**

This Covenant would not be like the Mosaic covenant. This time God who wrote His Law on stone would now write it upon hearts. Everyone who was involved in this covenant would know the Lord. They would know who God IS. Compare this with *1 John 5:20*.

God would be doing a new thing; He would be building a new creature. A person made with a new heart, a new Spirit and a brand new life. In fact God was referring to a new kind of human being; a person that was neither going to be classified as Jewish nor Gentile. This kind of individual would come to be known as a Christian.

Ezekiel 36:26 "*A new heart also will I give you, and a new spirit will I put within you: and I will take away the stony heart out of your flesh, and I will give you an heart of flesh.*
[27] And I will put my spirit within you, and cause you to walk in my statutes, and ye shall keep my judgments, and do them.
[28] And ye shall dwell in the land that I gave to your fathers; and ye shall be my people, and I will be your God."

> **A New Thing For Israel, God Will Make A New Covenant With Them. This Will Mean The Old One Must Go – It Will Cease To Be In Force.**

Here again God mentions the new covenant He will be making with the people of Israel. Now you may ask a question, what about the Gentiles? Well what about the Gentiles just think through it from the mind of God if you can for just a moment?

It would be pointless for God to say, "I'm going to make a new covenant with the Gentiles." Why? The Gentiles don't know anything about a covenant keeping God.

It would be totally pointless for God to even try to make a covenant with Gentiles until Gentiles know something about what it means to have a relationship with a covenant keeping God.

God didn't even make an old covenant with Gentiles. All the more reason why He shouldn't make a new covenant with Gentiles?

He had no relationship with anyone but the Jews outside of the fact that He is the Creator of all men. This then is the reason why there was no mention of Gentiles in relationship with God throughout the Old Testament.

It would have been pointless. It would have been like describing colours to a man born blind. Because the Gentiles did not know God; in order for them to know God, someone who knew Him would have to introduce them to Him.

To do this that someone would have to have God's consent and approval to do so. That would mean a new covenant would be needed to be the basis of a brand new relationship.

There would have to be a mediator of this new covenant between God and whomsoever He chose to make covenant with just as Moses was the mediator of the Old Covenant.

Who then would be the mediator of this new covenant between God and His covenant people Israel? Would this covenant be just between God and Israel?

Isaiah Chapter 42:1 reads, *"Behold my servant, whom I uphold; mine elect, in whom my soul delighteth; I have put my spirit upon him: <u>he shall bring forth judgment to the Gentiles</u>."*

Isiah 42:6 *"I the LORD have called thee in righteousness, and will hold thine hand, and will keep thee, and give thee for <u>a covenant of the people, for a light of the Gentiles;</u>"*

> **A New Thing for the Gentiles – Gentiles Get a Part in the New Covenant through Messiah**

Suddenly God is revealing a hidden plan; which is that it is messiah who is going to come will make a covenant with the Gentiles also, and He will be the mediator of this new covenant. In point of fact this very prophecy is referred to in the New Testament in ***Matthew 12:17-21***

It says the prophecy as written in the Old Testament should be interpreted *that "in his name shall the Gentiles trust."* That's how it came out in the New Testament in his name shall the Gentiles trust. This is uncanny, because later in scripture we find out that it is indeed His name that saves us, *Acts 2:38*.

Compare ***Luke 2:32*** *"A light to lighten the Gentiles, and the glory of thy people Israel."* This shows that Jesus would be the whole deal to everyone, whether they were Jews or Gentiles. Jesus is the Covenant maker and the Covenant keeper.

Isaiah 49 verse 8 again, God speaks about His messiah and says, "*Thus saith the LORD, In an acceptable time have I heard thee, and in a day of salvation have I helped thee: and I will preserve thee, and give thee for* **a covenant of the people**, *to establish the earth, to cause to inherit the desolate heritages;*" Check this against **2 Corinthians 6:2**

In **Isaiah 55** again speaking of the messiah, **Isaiah 55:3** "*Incline your ear, and come unto me: hear, and your soul shall live; and* <u>**I will make an everlasting covenant with you**</u>, *even the sure mercies of David.*

[4] Behold, I have given him for a witness to the people, a leader and commander to the people.

*[5] Behold<u>, **thou shalt call a nation that thou knowest not, and nations that knew not thee shall run unto thee**</u> because of the LORD thy God, and for the Holy One of Israel; for he hath glorified thee.*" Compare this with John 10:16.

The Bible calls Israel a nation and it calls the Gentiles nations or else it calls them heathens. It says that the messiah will go to the people who don't know him.

This was written to people like you and me, it was written to Gentiles. I always wondered what it meant when Christ said,"there's others of this fold that I have to bring in, other sheep of this fold"; the other sheep are the ones that didn't know him, it means the Gentiles.

So Jesus the Christ or the Messiah, He was to become the mediator of the new covenant. Here we have God speaking to Israel and saying, 'I am going to make a new covenant with you through Messiah.'

When He comes He shall bring this covenant and also He shall make this same Covenant with the Gentiles at the same time that it is made available to the Jews.

The Old Testament prophecies of the mediator who would establish this New Covenant with both Jews and Gentiles is about the making of the New Testament.

The New Testament is about God's love for mankind in action. God saw all mankind in need of a Saviour, not just the Jewish people.

However He chose to separate a man, and then a whole nation to Himself, because this would best serve His purpose of ultimately reconciling the whole world to Him.

From among this nation arise people who are taught the need for a Saviour, and commanded to share these truths with the whole world.

This good news gave all men access to God. The good news for all men was a matter of the love of God demonstrated. This good news comes through Messiah and must be believed by faith.

John 3:16 "*For God so loved the world, that he gave his only begotten Son, that whosoever believeth in him should not perish, but have everlasting life.*
[17] For God sent not his Son into the world to condemn the world;

but that the world through him might be saved.

[18] He that believeth on him is not condemned: but he that believeth not is condemned already, because he **hath not believed in the name** *of the only begotten Son of God"*

The Linking of the two Testaments

So let's go to the New Testament to the time when Jesus was *'breaking bread'* at the time of Passover. Let us recall the scene in the Old Testament where Moses when he dedicated the old covenant said *'this is the blood of the covenant'*, and he sprinkled the blood on the people.

In the New Testament when Jesus was at the last supper with His disciples He said, <u>**"break eat and take this cup and drink it for this is My blood of the New Testament, which is shared for many for the remission of sins**</u>*."* **Matthew 26:28.**

This is almost identical in every sense to what Moses said, in **Exodus 24:8**, when he was dedicating the Old Covenant: - *'the blood of the covenant'*.

The word 'Testament' is the same word, which means 'covenant'. The same Greek word is translated covenant 20 times and testament 13 time in the New Testament.

So the words 'New Testament' and the words 'New Covenant' mean the same thing it's a covenant just as Jesus spoke of in, *"***Mark 14:24** *'And he said unto them, This is my blood of the **new testament**, which is shed for many."* See also ***Luke 22:19-20; 1 Corinthians 11:23-27.***

Compare these with ***Isaiah 42:6 and Hebrews 7:22***, which says, that 'Jesus was made the surety of a better testament.' The word surety means He was made the guarantee or assurance.

He was the guarantee from the Old Testament. When it said: "He shall be a covenant to the people;" that meant that in the New Testament Jesus would personally be the guarantee for this new agreement. He Himself would be the 'manifested guarantee'. Physically he was to be both the hostage and the ransom money.

But how then were the Jews and Gentiles supposed to come together and become partners (joint heirs the Bible calls it) in this new agreement. It was a mystery to the prophets, they prophesied about it but they couldn't understand it.

It would seem that it is still pretty much a mystery today to many, because it is one of the most misunderstood subjects. If you think it's a well-understood subject, just take a look at the many denominations and splinter groups within denominations that have formed on the basis of a misinterpretation of the law.

We have already established that the vehicle that God would use to bring Jew and Gentile together under one covenant and one covenant keeping God, was to be what we today call 'the Church'.

Jesus said, **Matthew 16:18** *"And I say also unto thee, That thou art Peter, and upon this rock I will build my church; and the gates of hell shall not prevail against it."*

The Mystery once hid would be made plain. The Mystery in this situation was that God could make covenant with the Gentiles. It is a mystery that God could bring all peoples into a covenant together with Him.

The Jews we understand, but the Gentiles were God haters by nature and distant from God. This was truly a mystery and a miracle.

***Ephesians* 3:3** *"How that by revelation he made known unto me the mystery; (as I wrote afore in few words,*
[4] Whereby, when ye read, ye may understand my knowledge in the mystery of Christ)
[5] Which in other ages was not made known unto the sons of men, as it is now revealed unto his holy apostles and prophets by the Spirit;
[6] That the Gentiles should be fellowheirs, and of the same body, and partakers of his promise in Christ by the gospel:"

It isn't until you read and understand the book of Ephesians when Paul expounds what has been revealed to him through the Spirit of God, that we begin to understand that the mystery after His will is what we call the Church.

The church or the Ecclesia (the called out ones) to give it its proper name, is what God would use to 'call out' both Jews and Gentiles to come together for the first time in a covenant relationship on equal terms and conditions. There would be no middle wall of partition, no partiality, no preferential treatment.

The Jews would not get treated differently from the Gentiles. *"For in Christ Jesus there is neither Jew nor Greek for we are all one in Christ Jesus"*. In the church we have come from all nations, tribes and tongues to become one in Christ Jesus.

There is no distinction between Jews and Gentiles we have become one in the church and so you may then ask, well if this is the new covenant what happened to the old covenant, The Ten Commandments? Glad you asked that.

Well in **Ephesians Chapter 2**, we read, **Ephesians 2:11**

"*Wherefore **remember, that ye being in time past** Gentiles in the flesh, who are called **Uncircumcision by that which is called the Circumcision in the flesh made by hands**;*

*[12] That at **that time ye were without Christ**, being aliens from the commonwealth of Israel, and **strangers from the covenants of promise**, having no hope, and **without God in the world**:*

*[13] **But now in Christ Jesus** ye who sometimes were far off are **made nigh by the blood of Christ.***

*[14] For he is our peace, who **hath made both one**, and hath broken down the middle wall of partition between us;*

*[15] Having **abolished in his flesh the enmity, even the law of commandments contained in ordinances;** for to make in himself of twain **one new man**, so making peace; (read Colossians 2:20-22).*

*[16] And **that he might reconcile both unto God in one body** by the cross, having **slain the enmity thereby**:*

> *The one body it speaks of is the church - Romans 12:5; 1 Corinthians 12:12-13.*

Ephesians 2:17 And came and preached peace to you which were afar off, and to them that were nigh.

[18] For through him we **both have access by one Spirit** unto the Father.

[19] Now therefore ye are **no more strangers and foreigners, but fellowcitizens with the saints, and of the household of God;**

[20] And are **built upon the foundation of the apostles and prophets, Jesus Christ himself being the chief corner stone**;

[21] In whom all the building fitly framed together groweth unto an holy temple in the Lord:

[22] In whom ye also are **builded together for an habitation of God** through the Spirit."

The Bible uses the word abolish; now the Greek word for abolish means: - abolish, cease, destroy, do away with, become of none effect. From this we can say with assurance that,

> 'The birth of the New Covenant is meant by God to spell the death or end of the Old Covenant.'

The end of the Old Covenant and the beginning of the New Covenant

Remember in the Old Testament where God gave Moses the Ten Commandments written in stone the second time and how Moses came down with the Ten Commandments and his face shone.

Well in **2 Corinthians Chapter 3**, Paul is writing and under the inspiration of the Holy Spirit. He refers to the same passage of scripture about Moses in the Old Testament.

He looks on the church of the New Testament and applies that scripture about Moses by saying:

2 Corinthians 3:2 *"Ye are our epistle written in our hearts, known and read of all men: [3] Forasmuch as ye are manifestly declared to be the epistle of Christ ministered by us, written not with ink, but with the Spirit of the living God; **not in tables of stone, but in fleshly tables of the heart**."*

Thus fulfilling the prophecy in the Old Testament contained in **Jeremiah 31:31-34.**

Then he goes on to say **Corinthians II 3:6** *"Who also hath made us able ministers of the New Testament; not of the letter, but of the spirit: for the letter killeth, but the spirit giveth life."* Now listen carefully, *"But if the administration of death,"*

What is he calling the administration of death?

"Written and engraved in stone" now what was written and engraved in stone? The commandments of course! What all of them? Yes, all ten were glorious it was reflected glory that caused Moses' face to shine a bit like the glory the moon gets from the sun.

The Bible says, *"which glory was to be **done away**"*. Now this is the word of God, *"how shall not the ministration of the spirit be rather glorious"* or More like the sun itself. You see one covenant is a shadow and type of the real thing.

The first covenant is shown to be a mere reflection; the second being the substance and fulfilment of everything the first covenant promised. The second excels the first by far and is the real thing.

The whole of Second Corinthians chapter three needs to be read in its entirety, because this scripture is really telling us that one covenant (the Old Covenant) was the forerunner of the second and was like the journey, and not the destination.

The New covenant is the spiritual fulfilment of all the types and shadows of the Old covenant. The New Testament is where everything was supposed to go; it was and is the destination of all covenants. It is that 'better promise' of which Paul speaks in the book of Hebrews to explain.

Under the Old Testament, one had to commit the act of sin in order to be guilty, but in the New Testament if the thing is in your heart you are guilty already.

In the Old Testament this were prophesied and pointed to, but in the New Testament, the prophesies are fulfilled and expounded *Matthew 5, Colossians 2:16, 17.*

Some teach that the Ten Commandments are split into two categories, moral laws and ceremonial laws.

Then proceed to reason that the Lord has done away with the ceremonial but not the moral aspects of the law but not with the moral aspects of the Law.

Such a person continues by reasoning that the moral aspects of the law are still binding upon us but that the ceremonial aspects have been done away.

Through God's explanation, (such as the scripture above) we find that it is not just the ceremonial aspects of the Law that have been abolished, but 'the Law' in total. The complete covenant has been **'done away'** or **'abolished'**.

Corinthians II 4 And such trust have we through Christ to God-ward:

[5] Not that we are sufficient of ourselves to think any thing as of ourselves; but our sufficiency is of God;

*[6] Who also hath made us **able ministers of the new testament**; not of the letter, but of the spirit: for **the letter killeth,** but the spirit giveth life.*

*[7] But if the **ministration of death, written and engraven in stones,** was glorious, so that the **children of Israel could not stedfastly behold the face of Moses for the glory of his countenance; which glory was to be <u>done away</u>**:*

[8] How shall not the ministration of the spirit be rather glorious?

*[9] For if the **ministration of condemnation** be glory, much more doth the ministration of righteousness exceed in glory.*

[10] For even that which was made glorious had no glory in this respect, by reason of the glory that excelleth.

*[11] For if **that which is <u>done away</u> was glorious,** much more that which remaineth is glorious.*

[12] Seeing then that we have such hope, we use great plainness of speech:

*[13] And not as **Moses, which put a veil over his face,** that the **children of Israel could not stedfastly look to the end of that which is <u>abolished</u>**:*

*[14] But their minds were blinded: for until this day remaineth the same veil untaken away in the reading of the old testament; which veil is **<u>done away in Christ.</u>***

[15] But even unto this day, when Moses is read, the veil is upon their heart.

[16] Nevertheless when it shall turn to the Lord, the veil shall be taken away.

[17] Now the Lord is that Spirit: and where the Spirit of the Lord is, there is liberty.

[18] But we all, with open face beholding as in a glass the glory of the Lord, are changed into the same image from glory to glory, even as by the Spirit of the Lord."

Scripture says that the 'Old Testament had no glory in this respect', what respect is the Bible speaking of? It means in the sense, that if the first covenant was to be done away then you can't compare the first with the second.

The second is going to be forever and ever, so in that respect there is no comparison. *"For that which was* (it goes on to say) *done away"*. The thing that has been 'done with' has no standing before that which is permanent.

Scripture continues by speaking concerning certain people, who open these 'Ten Commandments' every day (the law) and they read what was abolished but had no power to change human hearts.

It says that the reason why they continue in what was abolished is because there is veil over their eyes (mind) so that they should not see or understand.

There is a veil over their heart (understanding) so that they cannot accept truth. People who trust in the Old Covenant have a veil covering their understanding so that they cannot see or perceive the glorious liberty of the New Covenant that we have in Christ Jesus.

Then the Bible goes on to say "But if they would turn away and turn their hearts to God then God will give them liberty.

Now the Lord is that spirit and where the spirit of the Lord is there is Liberty." Now that's a clear scriptural application, it speaks about when Moses came down with the veil over his face, and Paul used this scripture to prove that the Law was abolished.

Heart of the matter
While no one with biblical knowledge would dispute that there is moral foundation in the commandments, it is clear that in the New Testament period, God requires higher standards of moral conduct than under the Old Testament. It is not a moral versus ceremonial issue.

> **The issue is that God replaced the complete old covenant with a complete new covenant based upon better promises.**

Keeping the law in no way justifies us, because the law has in itself no capability to give us a higher standard of ethics.

Jesus said, *"it has been said of them of old time thou shalt not commit adultery but I say unto you he that looks at a woman and lusts after her in his heart has already committed adultery with her."*

Where? 'In his heart'. I believe it was for this reason that God decided to deal with the problem from its source. Jesus observed in scripture that the source of all sin is the heart - **Mark 7:18-23.**

Mark 7:18 "And he saith unto them, Are ye so without understanding also? Do ye not perceive, that whatsoever thing from without entereth into the man, it cannot defile him;
*[19] Because it **entereth not into his heart**, but into the belly, and goeth out into the draught, purging all meats?*
[20] And he said, That which cometh out of the man, that defileth the man.
*[21] For from within, **out of the heart of men**, proceed evil thoughts, adulteries, fornications, murders,*
[22] Thefts, covetousness, wickedness, deceit, lasciviousness, an evil eye, blasphemy, pride, foolishness:

[23] All these evil things come from within, and defile the man."

What Jesus is trying to show is that **sin begins in the heart**, and though the law can stop you from the act of sin through the threat of sanction, it in no way deals with the origin of sin. It in no way affects where sin arises from, because people can still be 'killing us' in their heart.

What Jesus said in effect was, 'if you say you hate your brother, you kill him already', But He had already notified us in scripture that He knew that the law said; *'thou shalt not murder'*.

What He is really asserting is that He was going to give us a higher standard by which to live. John says, "he that hates his brother is a murderer". This is a higher requirement than simply 'thou shall not kill'. All of the requirements of the New Testament are higher than those required by the law. They are not just simply higher, but different.

Different, because they have a different purpose. One has the purpose of leading you to the knowledge of the need for a Saviour, and the other the purpose of introducing you to that Saviour.

Therefore by accepting that the law is not an instrument of salvation but simply a guide, teacher and foreshadow; by this thought pattern, we establish the law and equip those we meet with how to tackle the sin in their hearts.

Romans 3:19 *"Now we know that what things soever the law saith, it saith to them who are under the law: that every mouth may be stopped, and all the world may become guilty before God.*

[20] Therefore by the deeds of the law there shall no flesh be justified in his sight: for by the law is the knowledge of sin.

[21] But now the righteousness of God without the law is manifested, being witnessed by the law and the prophets;

[22] Even the righteousness of God which is by faith of Jesus Christ unto all and upon all them that believe: for there is no difference:

[23] For all have sinned, and come short of the glory of God;

[24] Being justified freely by his grace through the redemption that is in Christ Jesus:

[25] Whom God hath set forth to be a propitiation through faith in his blood, to declare his righteousness for the remission of sins that are past, through the forbearance of God;

[26] To declare, I say, at this time his righteousness: that he might be just, and the justifier of him which believeth in Jesus.

[27] Where is boasting then? It is excluded. By what law? of works? Nay: but by the law of faith.

[28] Therefore we conclude that a man is justified by faith without the deeds of the law.

[29] Is he the God of the Jews only? is he not also of the Gentiles? Yes, of the Gentiles also:

[30] Seeing it is one God, which shall justify the circumcision by faith, and uncircumcision through faith.

[31] Do we then make void the law through faith? God forbid: yea, we establish the law."

Establishing the law gives us an understanding of **'the sin issue'**. This means that people do need a saviour to save them from sin. This can only happen beyond the confines of the law.

So when we accept Christ Jesus through faith we rise above the law and break into the arena of faith. Through faith we go to a place where no one is justified by the deeds of the law, we come to a place where Jesus alone is the Justifier and final destination of all faith in God.

Romans 10:1 *"Brethren, my heart's desire and prayer to God for Israel is, that they might be saved.*

[2] For I bear them record that they have a zeal of God, but not according to knowledge.

[3] For they being ignorant of God's righteousness, and going about to establish their own righteousness, have not submitted themselves unto the righteousness of God.

[4] For Christ is the end of the law for righteousness to every one that believeth."

Christ is the end of the law to everyone that believes. Christ takes you above sin to when you believe in Him, obey Him and follow Him by faith. *"For as many as are led by the spirit of God they are the sons of God"*. When you are a Son of God you walk above sin.

We walk above sin because we walk in the Spirit, and are led by the Spirit and by the same token, we become Sons of God through this process.

Sin is only able to entrap those who are justified by their works but when you are following God, His Spirit will lead you away from and above sin. He will give you power to walk right and become a mature child of God.

John 1:11 *He came unto his own, and his own received him not.*

[12] *But as many as received him, to them* ***gave he power to become the sons of God, even to them that believe on his name****:*

In the New Testament period, the attitude of heart and state of heart is more important to God that the commission or omission of the Law, **Romans 3:20-22.**

Since the heart of the matter in the New Testament is the heart; refraining from work for one day taken in isolation cannot be considered a moral act, as it has nothing to do with a man's character. Neither is it central to the subject of Salvation.

Why the law?
The law shows man the depth of his lawlessness. His conscience tells him when he is doing wrong, but the law shows him just how wrong he is.

1. **The law shows us our guilt before God and stops us from justifying ourselves.**

    Romans 3:19 "*Now we know that what things soever the law saith, it saith to them who are under the law: that every mouth may be stopped, and all the world may become guilty before God.*"

2. **The law brings to us the knowledge of sin.**

   Romans 3:20 *"Therefore by the deeds of the law there shall no flesh be justified in his sight: for by the law is the knowledge of sin"*

3. **Through the law sin is identified and becomes exceedingly sinful.**

   Romans 7:13 *"Was then that which is good made death unto me? God forbid. But sin, that it might appear sin, working death in me by that which is good; that sin by the commandment might become exceeding sinful."*

   After the knowledge of sin there must needs be a conviction of sin. Instead of trying to keep the law, we need to allow the Holy Ghost to work in our lives, to develop deep conviction for our sins.

4. **The law defines sin - Man didn't know what sin was until the law told us.**

   Romans 7:7 *"What shall we say then? is the law sin? God forbid. Nay, I had not known sin, but by the law: for I had not known lust, except the law had said, Thou shalt not covet."*

   Romans 6:14 *"For sin shall not have dominion over you: for ye are not under the law, but under grace."*

   The scriptures confirm that we are not under the law, but under grace. We are under a better covenant and not under the old covenant of the law.

   Sin should not have dominion over us, because we are not under the law. In ***Romans 6*** we are to not serve sin, but instead we are to live righteously.

Romans chapter 7 concludes that many Christians find it impossible to live life righteously (why - because its life under the law). We do not live the overcoming life by the 'trying to accomplish', of the flesh; but by the yielding of the spirit. This is why Paul insists that the commandment is holy and just.

Romans 7:12 "Wherefore the law is holy, and the commandment holy, and just, and good."

5. **The law cannot make anything perfect - though it is good and perfect.**

   Hebrews 7:19 "For the law made nothing perfect, but the bringing in of a better hope did; by the which we draw nigh unto God".

6. **The law is not made for a righteous man, but for the sinner.**

   1 Timothy 1:9 "Knowing this, that the law is not made for a righteous man, but for the lawless and disobedient, for the ungodly and for sinners, for unholy and profane, for murderers of fathers and murderers of mothers, for manslayers,

   [10] For whoremongers, for them that defile themselves with mankind, for menstealers, for liars, for perjured persons, and if there be any other thing that is contrary to sound doctrine;"

7. **What purpose does the law serve? It was added till the seed to whom the promise was made should come, it was an afterthought.** *Galatians 3:19*

   The apostle Paul in Galatians indicates the temporary nature of the law in the above passage. The law was given until Christ (the seed) should come.

   We would be kept under the law until the faith which would afterward should be revealed and become operative in our lives. In other words, we are under the law till we come to know Jesus.

8. **The law was not meant to give life, spiritual or otherwise,** *Galatians 3:21.* It was impossible for this to be the case because of the weaknesses of humankind. If it were possible that righteousness could have come by this means, then the death of Christ would have been unnecessary.

9. **The law was designed for the very purpose of bringing men and women to Christ.**

   Galatians 3:24 "*Wherefore the law was our schoolmaster to bring us unto Christ, that we might be justified by faith.*"

So what the scripture teaches us is that the law was troublesome to the fleshly nature of man, but nevertheless the law was good, because the law (Ten Commandments) showed us what was sin.

The Bible told us in *Galatians Chapter 3* that '*the Law was our schoolmaster to lead us to Christ, but that now Christ has come we are no longer under the schoolmaster.*'

What is a schoolmaster? The Law! You can't get it much clearer than that. Never forget the Law has a purpose. Even today it has a purpose and a role in the plan of God. The **Law was given to reveal and identify sin.** If we would preach the law more in evangelistic services, we would see more conversions.

The law convicts mankind of sin, righteousness and Judgement. If the scriptures had not said, 'thou shalt not covet', we wouldn't know that coveting is sin. But it does and we do.

10. **The law was designed to confirm what God has already written upon our hearts.** He gave the consciousness that all were sinners and therefore all needed a Saviour.

Psalms 19:7 "*The law of the LORD is perfect, converting the soul: the testimony of the LORD is sure, making wise the simple.*"

Romans 2:15 "*Which show the work of the law written in their hearts, their conscience also bearing witness, and their thoughts the mean while accusing or else excusing one another;)*"

God's law is written on the heart of every man. When we hear the law, it confirms what man already knows in his heart.
The law leaves us helpless; it neither aids nor assists us in or quest to overcome sin.

The law simply proves to us that we are helpless to deal with the sin problem by ourselves. It proves that unless we get help, we are doomed to failure and condemnation. As a sinner we were ignorant of the standard, certainty and the severity of God's judgement.

The good news of Jesus' suffering for our sins made no sense to our carnal minds, why? Because we had no idea of what the law demanded of us. We did not understand the holiness of God. We did not truly grasp the weight of 'Eternal Condemnation' as implied by the law.

As sinners each of us must be confronted with the consequences of our sins because of the ignorance that pervades our society concerning the law, such ignorance as will leave 'the sinner' careless for his soul, and standing before a just God without any recourse.

Only when we understand the severity of the sentence, and hear the prison doors of judgement slam behind us, are we in a frame of mind to accept the 'Good News'.

It is only when we are at the point of utter desperation that we truly appreciate grace. Before we can appreciate love, mercy and grace, we must understand sin, law and judgment. This is the purpose of the Law to help us to appreciate the Grace of God that is ours through the Gospel.

Galatians 3:10 *"For as many as are of the works of the law are under the curse: for it is written, Cursed is every one that continueth not in all things which are written in the book of the law to do them".*

Galatians 5:3 *"For I testify again to every man that is circumcised, that he is a debtor to do the whole law."*

James 2:10 *"For whosoever shall keep the whole law, and yet offend in one point, he is guilty of all"*

The testimony of the scripture leads to one inevitable conclusion that it is impossible to fulfil or please the standards set forth by the law without Christ. Everyone is bound to fail in at least one point, and almost certainly in others, and therefore be guilty of all; that path of failure leads to condemnation and death.

> **The inevitable conclusion is that the Ten Commandments as well as the rest of the Law has been done away and abolished**

CHAPTER 12

The limitation of the first covenant
Colossians 2:14 **Blotting out the handwriting of ordinances** *that was against us, which was contrary to us, and* **took it out of the way,** *nailing it to his cross;*

[15] And having spoiled principalities and powers, he made a show of them openly, triumphing over them in it.

[16] Let no man therefore judge you **in meat, or in drink, or in respect of an holyday, or of the new moon, or of the sabbath days***:*

[17] Which are a **shadow of things to come; but the body is of Christ***.*

Colossians Chapter 2 says that it was "blotted out" "the handwriting of the ordinances that was against us". When the Bible says they were blotted out it means it was wiped away.

It's the same word used when we talk about our sins being washed away or blotted out. Now there is no way that any believer amongst us will find it difficult to believe that God has wiped away our sins.

If we serve God in a confused covenantal relationship then our whole service is in vain because we are not going to be saved since we have no faith that God has wiped away our sins.

We must bear it in mind that it's by grace that we are saved, through the faith we display by our obedience to the revealed will of God.

For we who believe through Christ and Christ alone have not believed in vain but we do believe that when God says He wiped away all you sins that it is exactly what He means. He washed away all of your sins, they're washed away.

God used the same word when he describes the old covenant and the nature of the relationship of the Jews to Him under that covenant He says it was blotted out or washed away.

The old relationship or agreement is gone and that leaves the new. Not just for a small group of people, but for all mankind. Why? Because God so loved the World.

The Bible continues by saying that the law was "decayed". A strong word decayed. Listen to this scripture from **Hebrews 8 verse 7** says, "For if that first covenant was faultless, there should be no place else to look for a second."

Here the Bible acknowledges that <u>the first covenant wasn't faultless</u>, that's why God had to bring a second in to take its place. What then was the fault with the first covenant? What was wrong with it?

Well what was wrong with the first covenant, was that it couldn't remove sin; the blood of animals could not remove sin. It could not satisfy the wrath of God.

It could not change a man's heart. The first covenant could not give a man a clear conscience towards God. Every year they had to make a sacrifice, with it came a remembering of their sins.

Hebrews 9:15 *And for this cause he is the mediator of the new Testament, that by means of death, for the redemption of the transgressions that were under the first testament, they which are called might receive the promise of eternal inheritance.*
Hebrews 9:16 *For where a testament is, there must also of necessity be the death of the testator.*
Hebrews 9:17 *For a testament is of force after men are dead: otherwise it is of no strength at all while the testator liveth.*
Hebrews 9:18 *Whereupon neither the first testament was dedicated without blood.*

Hebrews 9:28 *So Christ was once offered to bear the sins of many; and unto them that look for him shall he appear the second time without sin unto salvation.*
Hebrews 10:1 *For the law having a shadow of good things to come, and not the very image of the things, can never with those sacrifices which they offered year by year continually make the comers thereunto perfect.*

The Jews were always looking in hope for that perfect day when the Messiah who would be known as the mediator of the New Testament would come and take away not only their sins, but the sins of those that had died under the Old Covenant looking for the coming of Messiah; unless Christ had died those that were under the Old Covenant would have been lost forever.

Every time they made a sacrifice to God with a Bull or a goat, it was an I.O.U that when Christ came His blood would wipe away all those sins. And so the scripture goes on to make it clear that God 'took away the first to establish the second'.

Hebrews 10:9 Then said he, Lo, I come to do thy will, O God.

He taketh away the first, that He may establish the second.

Hebrews 10:10 By the which will we are sanctified through the offering of the body of Jesus Christ once for all.

The Bible says that God took away the first Covenant and established the second so that what could not be accomplished by many sacrifices, would be done by one sacrifice once and for all. What was done through the sacrifice of Jesus will last forever.

If the first had stayed and the second had come there would have been competing covenants and confusion. Well since the purpose of the first was never to make man perfect, that was why God chose to do away with it. He replaced it with the new Covenant based upon better promises and with a better ending in sight.

The New Commandment

All of this information still does not tell us what we need to know about where the moral guidelines of the Church are given. So then how and where are the moral guidelines for the church clarified?

We have said what happened to the commandments, by this I mean 'the Ten Commandments'. This does not mean that we are without guide, without rule or lawless.

Let me put it this way, Jesus was asked what are the greatest of all the commandments; He was asked, "What must I do to obtain eternal life?"

The answer that He gave to both questions gives a strong clue as to what has happened to the old covenant if you do not understand by now.

He said, "Thou shalt love the Lord with all thy heart, they mind, with all they soul with all thy spirit and love thy neighbour as thyself."

Now those two scriptures are not from the Ten Commandment, neither one of them is from the Ten Commandments though they are contained in the law. These scriptures are quoted by Jesus from **Deuteronomy 6:4** and **Leviticus 19:18.** Notice the contrast here between this and the first commandment as recorded in the Ten Commandments in **Exodus 20:3.**

Jesus said, "upon these two commandments hang all the law and the prophets upon those two scriptures upon those two verses hang all the law and the prophets, Wow!

Now that's a strong statement because Jesus also said, "He did not come to destroy the law", that is because to destroy the law would be to destroy what the prophets said; for the prophets prophesied having the law as their foundation.

For us today what the prophets preached is a part of our foundation because we are to build upon the teaching of the prophets and the apostles keeping Jesus Christ as our chief cornerstone.

Jesus Christ said, "No! I did not come to destroy the law but I came to fulfil the law." Now that means that we also as the children of God have not come to destroy the law.

However neither have we come to keep it, but like Christ we must fulfil the law. How then can we fulfil the law? This is the next important step in our understanding

Fulfilling the Law

Many religious people of Jesus' day asked questions. Questions of concern for the application of the law. They did this not because they wanted an answer, but just to tempt him.

Some today will ask questions because they sincerely want an answer and others ask us questions simply to test us. "Oh you only keep nine?" No we don't keep the Old Testament we fulfil it. I want to show you that we don't keep but instead fulfil the old covenant.

Romans 13 verses 8 - 10 describes the five commandments that was given to man; don't lie, don't steal, don't bear false witness, don't covet, don't commit adultery, they were the five that pertained to man and he made us to know that love will work no ill to his neighbour therefore love is the fulfilling of the law.

Now God is a spirit and the very essence of God is love, God is love and therein is the connection to the new covenant? The essence of the New Covenant is Love. Stay with me a little longer it will become clear as we go along.

The Bible says that the love of God is shed abroad in our hearts by the Holy Ghost; so when God put His Spirit in us He put His love in us (and only God in Christ can ever fulfil the Law) therefore it is love that fulfils the law.

Love is the fulfilling of the law so when somebody ask you about the law or says what are you doing about the law, you say I am fulfilling the law because I have got the love of God in me.

What have you got in you? The Love of God? Only those who belong to the Apostolic Church (the Church Jesus started in the Bible) can fulfil the law whether Jew or Gentile, in the Church we are all one in Christ Jesus.

However we can only get into Christ Jesus by making covenant with Him according to the pattern shown us by the Apostles and disciples of Jesus Christ who became the dispensers of the New Covenant.

John 17:20 "Neither pray I for these alone, but for them also which shall believe on me through their (His Apostles) word;"

Now I want to show you something, Paul only mentions the five commandments that speak about man's responsibility to man. What about the other five that pertain to God? Well Jesus explained that when He said, "upon those two hang all the law and the prophets, you should love the Lord with all they heart, thy mind, thy body and thy Soul."

The apostle John speaking under the unction of the Holy Spirit in *1 John 3 verse 23-24* says something really profound. *"And this is his covenant that we should believe on the name of his son Jesus Christ and love one another as he gave us commandments."*

Is John missing it? Has he gone off the deep end when he summarises the New Covenant as believing on the name of Jesus and loving one another as He gave us commandment?

The explanation lies in the scripture where The Bible tells us that 'we ought to love the Lord with all our mind, all our heart, all our body, and all our soul and then love our neighbour as ourselves.'

Now John just comes along and appears at least at first to be contradicting that commandment which is the greatest commandment by saying, No! 'This is His command. The command that God has given us is that we should believe on the name of His son Jesus Christ and love one another as He gave us commandment.'

What is he saying? I am saying that, 'there is more to the name Jesus than a lot of us realise.' To believe on the name of the Lord Jesus Christ is the only way you can love God with all thy heart, all thy mind, all thy body and all thy soul.

That is why he placed that just like that, in other words the Apostolic Church is built on two laws, 'believe on the name of the law Jesus Christ and love thy neighbour as thyself.'

"This is the record that God has given to us eternal life and the life is in his son. He that have the son have life and he have not the Son of God have not life.

These things have I written onto you that believe on the name of the Son of God that ye may know that ye have eternal life and that ye may believe on the name of the Son of God."

By believing on the name of the Son of God, the Bible clearly says firstly, that is how we fulfil the law; secondly that the righteousness of the law is fulfilled in us who are the Church.

In the Old Testament in Deuteronomy, the Bible keeps calling the Ten Commandments the word of the covenant, he calls them the tables of the covenant and every time Moses refers to them this was the covenant that God gave to you. There's no way that you can separate the ten from the covenant.

So when Paul is speaking and he writes of the ordinances and the handwriting that were against us, predominant in his mind is the thought of the Ten Commandments or law. He called the ten that were given on Mount Sinai the ministration of death. He said they were engraved in stone.

God himself when prophesying through Jeremiah the prophet of the New Testament refers to that which was written in stone. He said He knew that the old covenant was written in stone but that this time He would write His laws in our hearts.

So you see we who are in the New Testament church don't keep but rather we fulfil God's commandments. The thought behind the commandments are simple, it is do or you die. Instead of trying to keep the commandments, we need to fulfil the commandments the only way it is possible for a man to please God.

We do that not because we have to and certainly not out of self-righteousness. We fulfil the law because He is in us and we love Him; you see when He said I'll put my spirit in you, God is love and because He put His Spirit in us He put His love in us, and love is the fulfilling of the law.

So through God's love we now fulfil the righteousness, which God demanded through the law and which, no man could fulfil; that is not any man except Jesus the Messiah.

Now since Messiah has come through Him we are able to satisfy God's demands that we have the righteousness, which He requires from everyone. So through Christ Jesus, that is faith in Christ Jesus, we now fulfil the law

> **Through Jesus we now fulfil the Law - Jesus alone is the way to fulfil the Commandments of God**

CHAPTER 13

THE SABBATH HOME BIBLE STUDY

In doing this Bible study, we will begin with two premises.

1. Everything that God does in scripture is based upon a principle and repeated in a pattern for our sure understanding. God never changes His principles, He only explains them.

2. The Sabbath is not an issue about what day, because that is a settled matter. The real issue that is causing problems is what covenant are we under today.

This study has been designed so that by a series of questions it is hoped that together we can investigate the Sabbath principle of the Word of God and arrive at the correct conclusion.

The meaning of Sabbath
1. What is the meaning of the word Sabbath? Rest!

> *Leviticus 23:3* Six days shall work be done: but the seventh day is **the sabbath of rest**, an holy convocation; **ye shall do no work** therein: it is the sabbath of the LORD in all your dwellings.

> *Exodus 23:12* Six days thou shalt do thy work, and **on the seventh day thou shalt rest**: that thine ox and thine ass may rest, and the son of thy handmaid, and the stranger, may be refreshed.

> *Exodus 16:30* So the people **rested** on the seventh day.

2. In the first mention of Sabbath in Genesis, is it presented as information or as a command to man that he should keep it? It is presented as information!

    > *Genesis 2:1* Thus the heavens and the earth were finished, and all the host of them.
    >
    > *Genesis 2:2* And on the seventh day God ended his work which he had made; and he **res**ted on the seventh day from all his work which he had made.
    >
    > *Genesis 2:3* And God blessed the seventh day, and sanctified it: because that in it he had rested from all his work which God created and made.

3. Where the Sabbath is mentioned for the first time in connection with mankind, is it given as information or as a law? It is presented as law or command!

    > *Exodus 16:22* And it came to pass, that on the sixth day they gathered twice as much bread, two omers for one man: and all the rulers of the congregation came and told Moses.
    >
    > *Exodus 16:23* And he said unto them, This is that which the LORD hath said, To morrow is the rest of the holy sabbath unto the LORD: bake that which ye will bake to day, and seethe that ye will seethe; and that which remaineth over lay up for you to be kept until the morning.

Exodus 16:24 *And they laid it up till the morning, as Moses bade: and it did not stink, neither was there any worm therein.*

Exodus 16:25 *And Moses said, Eat that to day; for to day is a sabbath unto the LORD: to day ye shall not find it in the field.*

Exodus 16:26 *Six days ye shall gather it; but on the seventh day, which is the sabbath, in it there shall be none.*

Exodus 16:27 *And it came to pass, that there went out some of the people on the seventh day for to gather, and they found none.*

Exodus 16:28 *And the LORD said unto Moses, How long refuse ye to keep my commandments and my laws?*

Exodus 16:29 *See, for that the LORD hath given you the sabbath, therefore he giveth you on the sixth day the bread of two days; abide ye every man in his place, let no man go out of his place on the seventh day.*

Exodus 16:30 *So the people rested on the seventh day.*

4. To whom is the Lord speaking at this point? Is He speaking to all mankind or to Israel? Israel!

5. At the formal explanation of the Sabbath given to Israel, to whom does God say He is giving the Sabbath as a sign (seal or evident proof) of His Covenant (agreement) with them? The Children of Israel!

Exodus 31:14 Ye shall keep the sabbath therefore; for it is holy unto you: every one that defileth it shall surely be put to death: for whosoever doeth any work therein, that soul shall be cut off from among his people.

Exodus 31:15 Six days may work be done; but in the seventh is the sabbath of rest, holy to the LORD: whosoever doeth any work in the sabbath day, he shall surely be put to death.

Exodus 31:16 Wherefore the children of Israel shall keep the sabbath, to observe the sabbath throughout their generations, for a perpetual covenant.

Exodus 31:17 It is a sign between me and the children of Israel for ever: for in six days the LORD made heaven and earth, and on the seventh day he rested, and was refreshed.

Exodus 31:18 And he gave unto Moses, when he had made an end of communing with him upon mount Sinai, two tables of testimony, tables of stone, written with the finger of God.

6. What did the Law require of those practising keeping a Sabbath day?

(a)   **Staying in their dwelling.**

Exodus 16:29 See, for that the LORD hath given you the sabbath, therefore he giveth you on the sixth day the bread of two days; abide ye every man in his place, let no man go out of his place on the seventh day.
Exodus 16:30 So the people rested on the seventh day.

(b) **Not kindling a fire.**

Exodus 35:3 Ye shall kindle no fire throughout your habitations upon the sabbath day.

(c) **Keeping every seventh year as a Sabbath.**

Exodus 23:10 And six years thou shalt sow thy land, and shalt gather in the fruits thereof:
Exodus 23:11 But the seventh year thou shalt let it rest and lie still; that the poor of thy people may eat: and what they leave the beasts of the field shall eat. In like manner thou shalt deal with thy vineyard, and with thy oliveyard.

(d) **Failure to keep the Sabbath resulted in the death of the Sabbath breakers.**

***Exodus* 35:2** *Six days shall work be done, but on the seventh day there shall be to you an holy day, a sabbath of rest to the LORD: whosoever doeth work therein shall be put to death.*

***Numbers* 15:32** *And while the children of Israel were in the wilderness, they found a man that gathered sticks upon the sabbath day.*

***Numbers* 15:33** *And they that found him gathering sticks brought him unto Moses and Aaron, and unto all the congregation.*

***Numbers* 15:34** *And they put him in ward, because it was not declared what should be done to him.*

***Numbers* 15:35** *And the LORD said unto Moses, The man shall be surely put to death: all the congregation shall stone him with stones without the camp.*

***Numbers* 15:36** *And all the congregation brought him without the camp, and stoned him with stones, and he died; as the LORD commanded Moses.*

***James* 2:10** *For whosoever shall keep the whole law, and yet offend in one point, he is guilty of all.*

7. **Are the 10 Commandments (the Law) and the Old Testament (Covenant) the same thing, or are they different?** The same thing!

Deuteronomy 4:12 *And the LORD spake unto you out of the midst of the fire: ye heard the voice of the words, but saw no similitude; only ye heard a voice.*

Deuteronomy 4:13 *And he declared unto you his covenant, which he commanded you to perform, even ten commandments; and he wrote them upon two tables of stone.*

Exodus 34:27 *And the LORD said unto Moses, Write thou these words: for after the tenor of these words I have made a covenant with thee and with Israel.*

Exodus 34:28 *And he was there with the LORD forty days and forty nights; he did neither eat bread, nor drink water. And he wrote upon the tables the words of the covenant, the ten commandments.*

8. **Has the Old Covenant (10 Commandments) been set aside for another Covenant? Yes, the New Testament/ Covenant!**

Hebrews 7:11 *If therefore perfection were by the Levitical priesthood, (for under it the people received the law,) what further need was there that another priest should rise after the order of Melchisedec, and not be called after the order of Aaron?*

Hebrews 7:12 *For the priesthood being changed, there is made of necessity a change also of the law.*
Hebrews 7:13 *For he of whom these things are spoken pertaineth to another tribe, of which no man gave attendance at the altar*

Hebrews 7:22 *By so much was Jesus made a surety of a better testament.*

Hebrews 8:7 *For if that first covenant had been faultless, then should no place have been sought for the second.*
Hebrews 8:8 *For finding fault with them, he saith, Behold, the days come, saith the Lord, when I will make a new covenant with the house of Israel and with the house of Judah:*

Hebrews 8:13 *In that he saith, A new covenant, he hath made the first old. Now that which decayeth and waxeth old is ready to vanish away.*

Hebrews 10:9 *Then said he, Lo, I come to do thy will, O God. He taketh away the first, that he may establish the second.*

2 Corinthians 3:6 *Who also hath made us able ministers of the new testament; not of the letter, but of the spirit: for the letter killeth, but the spirit giveth life.*

2 Corinthians 3:7 But if the ministration of death, written and engraven in stones, was glorious, so that the children of Israel could not stedfastly behold the face of Moses for the glory of his countenance; which glory was to be done away:

2 Corinthians 3:8 How shall not the ministration of the spirit be rather glorious?

2 Corinthians 3:9 For if the ministration of condemnation be glory, much more doth the ministration of righteousness exceed in glory.

2 Corinthians 3:10 For even that which was made glorious had no glory in this respect, by reason of the glory that excelleth.

2 Corinthians 3:11 For if that which is done away was glorious, much more that which remaineth is glorious.

2 Corinthians 3:12 Seeing then that we have such hope, we use great plainness of speech:

2 Corinthians 3:13 And not as Moses, which put a veil over his face, that the children of Israel could not stedfastly look to the end of that which is abolished:

2 Corinthians 3:14 But their minds were blinded: for until this day remaineth the same veil untaken away in the reading of the old testament; which veil is done away in Christ.

2 Corinthians 3:15 But even unto this day, when Moses is read, the veil is upon their heart.

2 Corinthians 3:16 Nevertheless when it shall turn to the Lord, the veil shall be taken away.

2 Corinthians 3:17 Now the Lord is that Spirit: and where the Spirit of the Lord is, there is liberty.

2 Corinthians 3:18 But we all, with open face beholding as in a glass the glory of the Lord, are changed into the same image from glory to glory, even as by the Spirit of the Lord.

9. **When was the Old Covenant (Old Testament) set aside? After its fulfilment by Jesus Christ through His death, burial and resurrection.**

Hebrews 9:15 And for this cause he is the mediator of the new testament, that by means of death, for the redemption of the transgressions that were under the first testament, they which are called might receive the promise of eternal inheritance.

Hebrews 9:16 For where a testament is, there must also of necessity be the death of the testator.

Hebrews 9:17 For a testament is of force after men are dead: otherwise it is of no strength at all while the testator liveth.

Hebrews 9:18 Whereupon neither the first testament was dedicated without blood.

Galatians 3:10 For as many as are of the works of the law are under the curse: for it is written, Cursed is every one that continueth not in all things which are written in the book of the law to do them.

Galatians 3:11 But that no man is justified by the law in the sight of God, it is evident: for, The just shall live by faith.

Galatians 3:12 And the law is not of faith: but, The man that doeth them shall live in them.

Galatians 3:13 Christ hath redeemed us from the curse of the law, being made a curse for us: for it is written, Cursed is every one that hangeth on a tree:

Galatians 3:14 That the blessing of Abraham might come on the Gentiles through Jesus Christ; that we might receive the promise of the Spirit through faith.

Hebrews 10:9 Then said he, Lo, I come to do thy will, O God. He taketh away the first, that he may establish the second.

Hebrews 10:10 By the which will we are sanctified through the offering of the body of Jesus Christ once for all.

Hebrews 10:11 And every priest standeth daily ministering and offering oftentimes the same sacrifices, which can never take away sins:

Hebrews 10:12 But this man, after he had offered one sacrifice for sins for ever, sat down on the right hand of God;

Hebrews 10:13 From henceforth expecting till his enemies be made his footstool.

Hebrews 10:14 For by one offering he hath perfected for ever them that are sanctified.

Hebrews 10:15 Whereof the Holy Ghost also is a witness to us: for after that he had said before,

Hebrews 10:16 This is the covenant that I will make with them after those days, saith the Lord, I will put my laws into their hearts, and in their minds will I write them;

Hebrews 10:17 And their sins and iniquities will I remember no more.

Hebrews 10:18 Now where remission of these is, there is no more offering for sin.

Hebrews 10:19 Having therefore, brethren, boldness to enter into the holiest by the blood of Jesus,

Hebrews 10:20 By a new and living way, which he hath consecrated for us, through the veil, that is to say, his flesh;

10. **Why did the law (Old Covenant) have to be set aside? Because its only the shadow and not the fulfilment of God's intent.**

Colossians 2:16 Let no man therefore judge you in meat, or in drink, or in respect of an holyday, or of the new moon, or of the sabbath days:

Colossians 2:17 Which are a shadow of things to come; but the body is of Christ.

John 7:16 Jesus answered them, and said, My doctrine is not mine, but his that sent me.

John 7:17 *If any man will do his will, he shall know of the doctrine, whether it be of God, or whether I speak of myself.*

John 7:18 *He that speaketh of himself seeketh his own glory: but he that seeketh his glory that sent him, the same is true, and no unrighteousness is in him.*

John 7:19 *Did not Moses give you the law, and yet none of you keepeth the law? Why go ye about to kill me?*

Hebrews 10:1 *For the law having a shadow of good things to come, and not the very image of the things, can never with those sacrifices which they offered year by year continually make the comers thereunto perfect.*

Galatians 6:12 *As many as desire to make a fair show in the flesh, they constrain you to be circumcised; only lest they should suffer persecution for the cross of Christ.*

Galatians 6:13 *For neither they themselves who are circumcised keep the law; but desire to have you circumcised, that they may glory in your flesh.*

Galatians 6:14 *But God forbid that I should glory, save in the cross of our Lord Jesus Christ, by whom the world is crucified unto me, and I unto the world.*

Galatians 6:15 *For in Christ Jesus neither circumcision availeth any thing, nor uncircumcision, but a new creature.*

11. **What does it mean to become a new creature? It means to be born again the way the Bible teaches in the book of Acts.**

Ephesians 2:13 But now in Christ Jesus ye who sometimes were far off are made nigh by the blood of Christ.

Ephesians 2:14 For he is our peace, who hath made both one, and hath broken down the middle wall of partition between us;

Ephesians 2:15 Having abolished in his flesh the enmity, even the law of commandments contained in ordinances; for to make in himself of twain one new man, so making peace;

Ephesians 2:16 And that he might reconcile both unto God in one body by the cross, having slain the enmity thereby:

Romans 13:8 Owe no man any thing, but to love one another: for he that loveth another hath fulfilled the law.

Romans 13:9 For this, Thou shalt not commit adultery, Thou shalt not kill, Thou shalt not steal, Thou shalt not bear false witness, Thou shalt not covet; and if there be any other commandment, it is briefly comprehended in this saying, namely, Thou shalt love thy neighbour as thyself.

Romans 13:10 Love worketh no ill to his neighbour: therefore love is the fulfilling of the law.

Romans 13:11 And that, knowing the time, that now it is high time to awake out of sleep: for now is our salvation nearer than when we believed.

Acts 2:38 *Then Peter said unto them, Repent, and be baptized every one of you in the name of Jesus Christ for the remission of sins, and ye shall receive the gift of the Holy Ghost.*

Acts 2:39 *For the promise is unto you, and to your children, and to all that are afar off, even as many as the Lord our God shall call.*

Acts 2:40 *And with many other words did he testify and exhort, saying, Save yourselves from this untoward generation.*

Acts 2:41 *Then they that gladly received his word were baptized: and the same day there were added unto them about three thousand souls.*

Romans 6:3 *Know ye not, that so many of us as were baptized into Jesus Christ were baptized into his death?*

Romans 6:4 *Therefore we are buried with him by baptism into death: that like as Christ was raised up from the dead by the glory of the Father, even so we also should walk in newness of life.*

Romans 6:5 *For if we have been planted together in the likeness of his death, we shall be also in the likeness of his resurrection:*

Romans 6:6 *Knowing this, that our old man is crucified with him, that the body of sin might be destroyed, that henceforth we should not serve sin.*

Romans 6:7 *For he that is dead is freed from sin.*

Romans 6:8 *Now if we be dead with Christ, we believe that we shall also live with him:*

Romans 6:9 *Knowing that Christ being raised from the dead dieth no more; death hath no more dominion over him.*

Romans 6:10 *For in that he died, he died unto sin once: but in that he liveth, he liveth unto God.*

Romans 6:11 *Likewise reckon ye also yourselves to be dead indeed unto sin, but alive unto God through Jesus Christ our Lord.*

13. **Were New Testament (New Covenant) believers meant to continue keeping the Law (which includes the Sabbath)? No because it has been superseded by the New Covenant!**

    Acts 15:7 *And when there had been much disputing, Peter rose up, and said unto them, Men and brethren, ye know how that a good while ago God made choice among us, that the Gentiles by my mouth should hear the word of the gospel, and believe.*

    Acts 15:8 *And God, which knoweth the hearts, bare them witness, giving them the Holy Ghost, even as he did unto us;*

    Acts 15:9 *And put no difference between us and them, purifying their hearts by faith.*

Acts 15:10 *Now therefore why tempt ye God, to put a yoke upon the neck of the disciples, which neither our fathers nor we were able to bear?*
Acts 15:11 *But we believe that through the grace of the Lord Jesus Christ we shall be saved, even as they.*
Acts 15:12 *Then all the multitude kept silence, and gave audience to Barnabas and Paul, declaring what miracles and wonders God had wrought among the Gentiles by them.*
Acts 15:13 *And after they had held their peace, James answered, saying, Men and brethren, hearken unto me:*
Acts 15:14 *Simeon hath declared how God at the first did visit the Gentiles, to take out of them a people for his name.*
Acts 15:15 *And to this agree the words of the prophets; as it is written,*
Acts 15:16 *After this I will return, and will build again the tabernacle of David, which is fallen down; and I will build again the ruins thereof, and I will set it up:*
Acts 15:17 *That the residue of men might seek after the Lord, and all the Gentiles, upon whom my name is called, saith the Lord, who doeth all these things.*

Acts 15:18 Known unto God are all his works from the beginning of the world.

Acts 15:19 Wherefore my sentence is, that we trouble not them, which from among the Gentiles are turned to God:

Acts 15:20 But that we write unto them, that they abstain from pollutions of idols, and from fornication, and from things strangled, and from blood.

Acts 15:28 For it seemed good to the Holy Ghost, and to us, to lay upon you no greater burden than these necessary things;

Acts 15:29 That ye abstain from meats offered to idols, and from blood, and from things strangled, and from fornication: from which if ye keep yourselves, ye shall do well. Fare ye well.

Acts 15:30 So when they were dismissed, they came to Antioch: and when they had gathered the multitude together, they delivered the epistle:

Acts 15:31 Which when they had read, they rejoiced for the consolation.

14. **How did Paul the Apostle view the Law including the Sabbath? He believed its not for the gentiles, it's a type shadow, a school master to lead us to Christ.**

Galatians 2:11 But when Peter was come to Antioch, I withstood him to the face, because he was to be blamed.

Galatians 2:12 For before that certain came from James, he did eat with the Gentiles: but when they were come, he withdrew and separated himself, fearing them which were of the circumcision.

Galatians 2:13 And the other Jews dissembled likewise with him; insomuch that Barnabas also was carried away with their dissimulation.

Galatians 2:14 But when I saw that they walked not uprightly according to the truth of the gospel, I said unto Peter before them all, If thou, being a Jew, livest after the manner of Gentiles, and not as do the Jews, why compellest thou the Gentiles to live as do the Jews?

Galatians 2:15 We who are Jews by nature, and not sinners of the Gentiles,

Galatians 2:16 Knowing that a man is not justified by the works of the law, but by the faith of Jesus Christ, even we have believed in Jesus Christ, that we might be justified by the faith of Christ, and not by the works of the law: for by the works of the law shall no flesh be justified

Galatians 4:9 But now, after that ye have known God, rather are known of God, how turn ye again to the weak and beggarly elements, whereunto ye desire again to be in bondage?

Galatians 4:10 Ye observe days, and months, and times, and years.

Galatians 4:11 I am afraid of you, lest I have bestowed upon you labour in vain

15. **What does Scripture teach about keeping a certain day holy? Scripture says its between you and God which day is holy and how many days you choose as special.**

Colossians 2:16 Let no man therefore judge you in meat, or in drink, or in respect of an holyday, or of the new moon, or of the sabbath days:

Colossians 2:17 Which are a shadow of things to come; but the body is of Christ.

Romans 14:5 One man esteemeth one day above another: another esteemeth every day alike. Let every man be fully persuaded in his own mind.

PTO Continued overleaf:

> ***Romans 14:6*** *He that regardeth the day, regardeth it unto the Lord; and he that regardeth not the day, to the Lord he doth not regard it. He that eateth, eateth to the Lord, for he giveth God thanks; and he that eateth not, to the Lord he eateth not, and giveth God thanks.*

16. **What then is the purpose of the Law? To show you that you cannot save yourself, but need a Saviour in the person of Jesus Christ.**

> ***Galatians 3:19*** *Wherefore then serveth the law? It was added because of transgressions, till the seed should come to whom the promise was made; and it was ordained by angels in the hand of a mediator.*
>
> ***Galatians 3:20*** *Now a mediator is not a mediator of one, but God is one.*
>
> ***Galatians 3:21*** *Is the law then against the promises of God? God forbid: for if there had been a law given which could have given life, verily righteousness should have been by the law.*
>
> ***Galatians 3:22*** *But the scripture hath concluded all under sin, that the promise by faith of Jesus Christ might be given to them that believe.*
>
> ***Galatians 3:23*** *But before faith came, we were kept under the law, shut up unto the faith which should afterwards be revealed.*
>
> ***Galatians 3:24*** *Wherefore the law was our schoolmaster to bring us unto Christ, that we might be justified by faith.*

Galatians **3:25** *But after that faith is come, we are no longer under a schoolmaster.*

Galatians **3:26** *For ye are all the children of God by faith in Christ Jesus.*

Galatians **3:27** *For as many of you as have been baptized into Christ have put on Christ.*

1 Corinthians 10:11 *Now all these things happened unto them for ensamples: and they are written for our admonition, upon whom the ends of the world are come.*

Romans 15:4 *For whatsoever things were written aforetime were written for our learning, that we through patience and comfort of the scriptures might have hope.*

17. **In what way does Jesus fulfil the Law (including the Sabbath)? Jesus is the fulfilment of the Law because He alone fulfilled all righteousness by living a perfect and sinless life. We therefore can only live a life pleasing to God through Christ Jesus who lives in us and gives us hope to make it to glory, "Christ in you the hope of glory".**

Romans 10:1 *Brethren, my heart's desire and prayer to God for Israel is, that they might be saved.*

Romans 10:2 *For I bear them record that they have a zeal of God, but not according to knowledge.*

Romans 10:3 *For they being ignorant of God's righteousness, and going about to establish their own righteousness, have not submitted themselves unto the righteousness of God.*

Romans 10:4 *For Christ is the end of the law for righteousness to every one that believeth.*

Colossians 2:17 *Which are a shadow of things to come; but the body is of Christ.*

Romans 4:8 *Blessed is the man to whom the Lord will not impute sin.*

Romans 4:9 *Cometh this blessedness then upon the circumcision only, or upon the uncircumcision also? for we say that faith was reckoned to Abraham for righteousness.*

Romans 4:10 *How was it then reckoned? when he was in circumcision, or in uncircumcision? Not in circumcision, but in uncircumcision.*

Romans 4:11 *And he received the sign of circumcision, a seal of the righteousness of the faith which he had yet being uncircumcised: that he might be the father of all them that believe, though they be not circumcised; that righteousness might be imputed unto them also:*

Romans 4:12 And the father of circumcision to them who are not of the circumcision only, but who also walk in the steps of that faith of our father Abraham, which he had being yet uncircumcised.

Romans 4:13 For the promise, that he should be the heir of the world, was not to Abraham, or to his seed, through the law, but through the righteousness of faith.

Romans 4:14 For if they which are of the law be heirs, faith is made void, and the promise made of none effect:

Romans 4:15 Because the law worketh wrath: for where no law is, there is no transgression.

Romans 4:16 Therefore it is of faith, that it might be by grace; to the end the promise might be sure to all the seed; not to that only which is of the law, but to that also which is of the faith of Abraham; who is the father of us all,

18. **Who or what is the meaning of true Sabbath in the New Testament? Our relationship with Jesus Christ is our peace with God, so our rest in Christ is the true meaning of Sabbath.**

Matthew 11:28 Come unto me, all ye that labour and are heavy laden, and I will give you rest.

Hebrews 4:7 *Again, he limiteth a certain day, saying in David, To day, after so long a time; as it is said, To day if ye will hear his voice, harden not your hearts.*

Hebrews 4:8 *For if Jesus had given them rest, then would he not afterward have spoken of another day.*

Hebrews 4:9 *There remaineth therefore a rest to the people of God.*

Hebrews 4:10 *For he that is entered into his rest, he also hath ceased from his own works, as God did from his.*

Hebrews 4:11 *Let us labour therefore to enter into that rest, lest any man fall after the same example of unbelief.*

Ephesians 1:13 *In whom ye also trusted, after that ye heard the word of truth, the gospel of your salvation: in whom also after that ye believed, ye were sealed with that holy Spirit of promise,*

Ephesians 1:14 *Which is the earnest of our inheritance until the redemption of the purchased possession, unto the praise of his glory*

Ephesians 4:30 *And grieve not the holy Spirit of God, whereby ye are sealed unto the day of redemption.*

Acts 5:30 *The God of our fathers raised up Jesus, whom ye slew and hanged on a tree.*

Acts 5:31 *Him hath God exalted with his right hand to be a Prince and a Saviour, for to give repentance to Israel, and forgiveness of sins.*

Acts 5:32 *And we are his witnesses of these things; and so is also the Holy Ghost, whom God hath given to them that obey him.*

19. **How will we know when we have received true Sabbath? When we have made peace with God by repentance, receiving the Holy Ghost and making our personal covenant with God through taking on His name.**

Isaiah 28:11 For with stammering lips and another tongue will he speak to this people.
Isaiah 28:12 To whom he said, This is the rest wherewith ye may cause the weary to rest; and this is the refreshing: yet they would not hear.

John 7:37 In the last day, that great day of the feast, Jesus stood and cried, saying, If any man thirst, let him come unto me, and drink.
John 7:38 He that believeth on me, as the scripture hath said, out of his belly shall flow rivers of living water.
John 7:39 (But this spake he of the Spirit, which they that believe on him should receive: for the Holy Ghost was not yet given; because that Jesus was not yet glorified.)

Mark 16:16 *He that believeth and is baptized shall be saved; but he that believeth not shall be damned.*

Titus 3:5 *Not by works of righteousness which we have done, but according to his mercy he saved us, by the washing of regeneration, and renewing of the Holy Ghost;*
Titus 3:6 *Which he shed on us abundantly through Jesus Christ our Saviour;*
Titus 3:7 *That being justified by his grace, we should be made heirs according to the hope of eternal life.*

Romans 5:5 *And hope maketh not ashamed; because the love of God is shed abroad in our hearts by the Holy Ghost which is given unto us.*

20. **Are we now without any laws to answer to in the New Testament period? No we do have a law, however it is simplified in that its called the royal law, and its all based around love for God. Because we love God, we show it by how we serve God.**

    1 Corinthians 9:19 *For though I be free from all men, yet have I made myself servant unto all, that I might gain the more.*
    1 Corinthians 9:20 *And unto the Jews I became as a Jew, that I might gain the Jews; to them that are under the law, as under the law, that I might gain them that are under the law;*

1 Corinthians 9:21 *To them that are without law, as without law, (being not without law to God, but under the law to Christ,) that I might gain them that are without law.*

Romans 13:8 *Owe no man any thing, but to love one another: for he that loveth another hath fulfilled the law.*

Romans 13:9 *For this, Thou shalt not commit adultery, Thou shalt not kill, Thou shalt not steal, Thou shalt not bear false witness, Thou shalt not covet; and if there be any other commandment, it is briefly comprehended in this saying, namely, Thou shalt love thy neighbour as thyself.*

Romans 13:10 *Love worketh no ill to his neighbour: therefore love is the fulfilling of the law.*

1 John 3:23 *And this is his commandment, That we should believe on the name of his Son Jesus Christ, and love one another, as he gave us commandment.*

1 John 3:24 *And he that keepeth his commandments dwelleth in him, and he in him. And hereby we know that he abideth in us, by the Spirit which he hath given us.*

CHAPTER 14

A QUESTION OF SABBATH

Here is a simple outline for the subject matter that can help you clarify and focus on the issues at hand:

Genesis 2:2-3   **First mention**

Exodus 16:23-30   The meaning of Sabbath and how to keep it

Exodus 20:8-11   Sabbath becomes a commandment to Israel

Exodus 23:10-12   Sabbath extends to the land

Exodus 31:12-18   God confirms His intent, confirmed who should keep it, confirmed penalty for breaking it, confirmed we are talking about an aspect of the 10 commandments.

Exodus 32:15-16   Tables of testimony written on stones?

Exodus 34:27-28   The covenant made with Israel written upon the tables of stone is the Law.

Exodus 35:2-3   One thing that should not be done on the Sabbath.

Leviticus 23:3   Where Sabbath was to be celebrated

Leviticus 23:23-32   Another Sabbath

*Leviticus 23:38   There is more than one Sabbath

Leviticus 25:2-17   Sabbath extends to the land

*Numbers 15:32-36   How they dealt with Sabbath breakers

Deut'y 5:12-15   Why Israel was to keep the Sabbath

*Deut'y 10:1-4   The law, the covenant & the ten commandments are the same.

(Deut'my = Deuteronomy)

Isaiah 1:13-19	God is upset because of Israel's lack of commitment to obedience to His Covenant.
Isaiah 56:1-8	A promise to those that keep His covenant, whether of the house of Israel or strangers.
Isaiah 58:13-14	A promise to Israel concerning fasting
Isaiah 66:20-23	A promise for the kingdom age
*Jeremiah 17:21-24	The Jews break the covenant and punishment is promised v 27.
*Lamentations 2:6	Punishment fulfilled
Ezekiel 20:12-26	God explains His actions
Ezekiel 20:36-44	God explains the remedy

Matthew 11:28-30 True Sabbath is a person not a day. Isa 28:11-12.

Matthew 12:1-8 The Lord of the Sabbath is here

Matthew 12:10-14 Jesus reinterprets their version of Sabbath keeping He healed on the Sabbath day.

Luke 4:31 He taught them on the Sabbath days

Luke 13:14-17 The doctors of the Law were shamed by his teachings of the Sabbath.

John 5:9-18 They understood that even picking up your bed was work – His claims frightened them.

John 9:14-16 Jesus does more miracles to upset their doctrine. Why?

Acts 15:5-11 A question of law, is a question of faith up for discussion in the New Testament period.

Acts 15:22-29   What gentile believers should keep to be saved.

Romans 13:9-14   The emphais is the Law of Love more about that later. James 2:8-12.

Romans 14:1-7   Those of weaker faith

**2 Corinthian 3:3-18* The law is done away in Christ

Galatians 3:1,9-14   A warning to the law keeper and the law breaker.

**Galatians 3:22-27*   The purpose of the law to bring us to Christ.

Galatians 4:8-11   Does this sound familiar? Isa. Ch 1?

**Ephesian 2;15 — 20*   The law abolished when Christ died.

**Colossians 2:10-17* The Sabbaths & holidays were simply a type of the real thing that is in Christ.

1Timothy 1:5-11   The law was never meant for a righteous man but for sinners.

Hebrews 3:6-4 & 1-11   Enter into rest! Can you remember who is our rest?

Hebrews 8:5-13   Confirmation that the Old testament or covenant was done away.

Hebrews 9:14-22   The final covenant has been made we have peace with God through Jesus - Rom 5:1.

> **We can clearly say, that we are not under the law of the 10 Commandments, but rather we have a new law written on our hearts which is the law of love.**

The Law of Moses (including the Ten Commandments) was written for the Jews (Israel) and was only to last until the time of Christ. In the Law of Moses, the blood of animals was required to atone for the sins of the people. These sacrifices were temporary.

ALSO AVAILABLE FROM DR UDENNIS

6" x 9" (15.24 x 22.86 cm)
Black & White on White paper
278 pages
Easyrway ltd
ISBN-13: 978-0956490605
ISBN-10: 0956490603
BISAC: Religion / Education

This book is the result of wanting to be healed without pills and potions. It is a journey of discovery about what it takes to live a healthier life based on wholesome food, exercise and some knowledge of herbal remedies. This book arises out of a sincere desire to be understand, be understood and also be respected by my doctor, such that I felt qualified in knowing my body and being able to say - no to the doctor.

WWW.DrTrevorUdennis.com

The 10 Commandments for everyday living

"No to the doctor Seminar"

This one day seminar/ Workshop includes:
- Information on God's lifestyle for man
- What we eat that poisons us
- What we should eat
- How exercise helps us
- The beauty of water
- Fresh air and fresh mindset

For Information about the, "No to the doctor Seminar/ workshop"

Visit: www.DrTrevorUdennis.com

"The Sabbath Seminar"

This one day seminar/ Workshop includes:
- Information on what the Sabbath keepers think
- Where the error of Sabbath began for Christians
- Why its such a prevalent false doctrine
- How to truly apply the Law to everyday living
- How to correctly apply the teaching of Sabbath to your life today.
- How to ensure you have true Sabbath

For Information about the, "Sabbath Seminar / workshop"

Visit: www.DrTrevorUdennis.com

The 10 Commandments for everyday living

www.ingramcontent.com/pod-product-compliance
Lightning Source LLC
LaVergne TN
LVHW051549070426
835507LV00021B/2484